Waggy

The Ken Wagstaff Story

Waggy

The Ken Wagstaff Story

John Maffin

Foreword by Sir Tom Courtenay

TEMPUS

Dedication

This book is dedicated to the memory of Raich Carter, the guiding light throughout my football career. He was a wonderful role model, brilliant mentor and an eternal beacon of hope.

Ken Wagstaff

September 2002

First published 2002, reprinted 2002

PUBLISHED IN THE UNITED KINGDOM BY:
Tempus Publishing Ltd
The Mill, Brimscombe Port
Stroud, Gloucestershire GL5 2QG

PUBLISHED IN THE UNITED STATES OF AMERICA BY:
Tempus Publishing Inc.
2 Cumberland Street
Charleston, SC 29401

British Library Cataloguing in Publication Data.
A catalogue record for this book is available from the British Library.

ISBN 0 7524 2732 6

Typesetting and origination by Tempus Publishing.
Printed in Great Britain by Midway Colour Print, Wiltshire

Contents

Ken Wagstaff, October 1966.

Foreword
by Sir Tom Courtenay

It was my dad who first got me excited about Waggy. 'Wait till you see our new player. He gets the ball, runs up the field and scores,' he exclaimed on the phone. I first saw him on an icy pitch at Millwall. City lost 3-0. I don't think they thought the match should have been played. But it wasn't long before Waggy and his legendary partner Chris Chilton were unfurled in all their glory and I used to talk about them wherever I went. Omar Sharif heard a great deal about them. We used to get the production manager on *The Night of The Generals* to phone the Hull City score service from Paris. And I remember Paddy Crerand telling me at Old Trafford that he thought they were the best pair of strikers in the League.

I had to be careful watching away matches with dignitaries. At Luton, Eric Morecambe invited me at half-time (0-0 but Luton on top) to have a drink in the inner sanctum after the game. Waggy nicked a goal in the second half and City won. 'I'm not gloating,' I said to Eric, but he knew I was (couldn't help myself) and the atmosphere was strained.

I remember City beating Watford at Vicarage Road. Waggy bagged one goal and one assist, as did Chillo. I was sitting with Dad in the Directors' Box. At the first goal, I stood up and shouted, 'Yes!' There was silence all around me and a lot of baleful looks. At the second goal Dad put a restraining hand on my arm. 'We mustn't look too pleased,' he said. 'Not in the Directors' Box.'

The best away match of all was when City played Chelsea in the Cup at Stamford Bridge – though it was on my doorstep. All my London pals were ready to give me a very hard time. Chelsea were two up and annihilation looked to be on the cards, but City didn't give in. John Maffin describes the unfolding drama in Chapter One. All I will say here is that what made it great for Dad and me was that Len Hutton and his son Richard, who I'd met with the Yorkshire team (in Hollywood would you believe), were sitting a few rows behind us and gave us a wave. I thought Dad's chest would burst with pride as we waved back. When we got home to my house in Fulham somebody had pinned a black and amber rosette on the front door.

Dad loved the way Waggy looked as though he was enjoying playing and wasn't afraid to laugh on the pitch. He liked his 'kidology' as he called it. 'He's a better actor than you are,' Dad once said during the game. He was thrilled to meet Waggy and have a drink with him. Once we all played Monopoly at my sister's house and Dad laughed all the way through – especially when he caught Waggy robbing the bank.

When I was the subject of *This Is Your Life* I was ushered to a posh house in Mayfair. I expected to meet an Italian film director, but to my astonishment there were Tommy Kavanah, Malcolm Lord and then Waggy holding a football and grinning from ear to ear. The mystery was solved when Eamon Andrews put his head round the corner. In fact, had Waggy not scored the only goal in a cup tie against Coventry the previous Saturday, they wouldn't have been there at all. They'd have been involved in a replay. Trust Waggy not to want to miss a good night.

So all those goals and a wonderful sense of playing for fun. There's not much of that nowadays.

Duel in the snow. Hull City inside right Ken Wagstaff and Grimsby right back Jimmy Thompson tussle for possession in a Humberside Derby at Boothferry Park on 27 November 1965.

Acknowledgements

This volume would not have been possible without the close co-operation of Ken Wagstaff, his family and an amazing array of friends – in football, show business and other walks of life.

In particular, I would like to thank former Hull City and Mansfield Town footballer David Coates for his wonderful memories. Invaluable input came from former Stags players Peter Morris, Michael Stringfellow, Sammy Chapman and Brian Phillips. Former Mansfield player and long-serving secretary Joe Eaton provided unique behind-the-scenes insights of Ken's Mansfield days for which I am immensely grateful.

All of Waggy's former colleagues at Hull City were extremely generous with their time. In particular, my gratitude goes to: Andy Davidson, Chris Chilton, Ian McKechnie, Chris Simpkin, John McSeveney, Ray Henderson, John Kaye, Ken Houghton, Ian Butler, Doug Clarke, Malcolm Lord, Roger De Vries and Mick Brown. Special thanks are also due to Alan Plater and Sir Tom Courtenay.

I am also grateful to the *Hull Daily Mail* and the *Mansfield Chad* for allowing access to their archives and for their kind permission to reproduce some of their wonderful pictures in this work. Author and Hull City historian Mike Peterson was a source of essential information and match statistics on Hull City Football Club. The same thanks are due to Mansfield Town historians Paul Taylor and Martin Shaw.

For those who are not specifically mentioned here, the book remains a testimony and a tribute to their contribution as Waggy's friends and team-mates in the unfolding dramas. Without the influence of the late Raich Carter on the career of Ken Wagstaff, this book may never have been written. To Pat and the family, I extend my warm thanks for their kind co-operation and help.

In a wider sense, I would like to thank those special people in my life who have provided me with the inspiration to write.

For in her eyes, I saw the words
As if she herself had spoken
And as they flowed I felt her there
Our spirits still unbroken
Her loving touch and gentle smile
In every road and lane
For what we were I give her this –
A Melody Unchained

John Maffin
September 2002

Waggy on the ball heading towards the goal, August 1967.

Introduction

Ken Wagstaff was a rare football talent. Born in the mining village of Langwith, he grew up with a ball forever at his feet. As a teenager, he played in the Nottinghamshire minor leagues for Langwith BC and the Imps. Despite his prolific goalscoring record, it was only by chance that he was spotted by Mansfield Town manager and ex-England International legend Raich Carter.

In 1960, Waggy signed for the Stags and embarked on a professional career that would eventually bring him to the brink of International honours. Indeed, in 1971 he toured Australasia with the FA in company of his talented Hull City strike partner Chris Chilton.

After almost five seasons at Field Mill, which saw the team rise into Division Three, the young goal ace became the centre of transfer speculation with the country's top clubs leading the chase for his services. In the end, it was ambitious Division Three side Hull City that secured his signature for the then princely sum of £40,000. At Boothferry Park, with reliability, style, speed and guile, he continued to weave his way through defences with ease. A cool finisher, he was able to read the game and create countless chances for others. Within the space of a season, the Tigers were promoted and became an exciting force in Division Two.

In the years that followed and under several managers – including Cliff Britton, Terry Neil and John Kaye – he blazed a free-scoring trail and broke a string of records on the way. In 1966 sections of the media bayed for him to be included in the England World Cup squad, but full International honours eluded him. Finally, the effect of accumulated injuries forced his retirement from major competitions – his swan song being a successful period as player/manager of George Cross in Australia and a later involvement in local coaching in the Hull area.

Whenever contemporaries of the era talk about football, whether they come from Mansfield or Hull, the name of Ken Wagstaff is never far from their lips. He became a legend in the hearts of those fans that saw him in action. His strike partnership with Chris Chilton was nothing short of sensational.

In his career, Ken Wagstaff made many friends. Some were stars in their own right and many were from other fields. Their vivid recollections and hilarious tales form a golden thread woven through this record. Waggy was an icon in his day – a man of great character, exceptional talent and steely determination.

This is his story.

John Maffin
August 2002

1

All in the Game

26 March 1966. Stamford Bridge – a stadium packed with 46,324 excited and passionate football fans. It was Hull City versus Chelsea – a contest between Division Three's high flyers and the cream of Division One in the sixth round of the FA Cup. The atmosphere was electric.

In the crowd was Len Hutton, the Yorkshire and England cricket legend. Close by was Hull-born actor Tom Courtenay – star of the film *Dr Zhivago*. Alongside, sat adopted City fan Rodney Bewes of television's *Likely Lads* fame. In the face of smiles from his other 'London friends', Courtenay hoped that his beloved team could upset the Chelsea apple cart.

Already, the brave Tigers had dumped Southampton and Nottingham Forest out of the competition. The stakes were getting ever higher. As the twin towers of Wembley beckoned still closer, the gathered audience waited expectantly to witness the nail-biting contest about to unfold before their eyes. This was to be no gentleman's wicket, no comedy episode or romantic film with breathtaking snow scenes. Instead, it was live sporting drama on a grand scale. On this set and on this day, amid a galaxy of talent on the pitch, which of the performers would win football's man-of-the-match Oscar?

As kick off approached, tension was high in the dressing room as the players prepared to stride into a cauldron of noise. Yet, amid the butterflies and tingling nerves, the Hull side brimmed with confidence and self-belief. Although Division One Chelsea had nine Internationals on the field, many observers felt that, man for man, Hull were far from an inferior side. Importantly, the team believed they could reach Wembley and lift the FA Cup for the first time in their history.

In goal for City, Maurice Swan was considered an extremely safe pair of hands. Long-serving Andy 'Jock' Davidson always provided stability and strong leadership on the field. His full-back partner Dennis Butler was a former Chelsea player. Together, they held a solid line. Essentially playing a 4-4-2 formation, the Tigers had a supremely creative player in Ken Houghton, with winger Ian Butler providing powerful runs and sharp crosses.

Chris Simpkin was a commanding player in midfield. His incisive tackling and pene-trating moves caused havoc for defenders. For Chris, the match at Chelsea was a special day. He'd always wanted to become a professional footballer and had always yearned for the big stage. Born within sight of the Boothferry Park ground, he'd once disclosed to his headmaster that his ambitions lay in the game and not in academic pursuits. That frankness earned him the cane. This game was the pinnacle of his career so far. Would the dream come true – or turn into a nightmare?

Alan Jarvis formed the other half of the attacking wing-half combination. A solid reliable influence in midfield, the budding Welsh International was relishing the chance to perform against top-flight opposition. The moment was nigh.

FA Cup action at Boothferry Park, 12 February 1966 – Hull City 2-0 Nottingham Forest.

As the minute hand of the dressing-room clock arced towards kick-off time, City's players changed into their amber and black match kit. The manager was ever calm and confident. It worked wonders.

For inside forward Ray Henderson this was a big day, but one for which he was well prepared. As a schemer and right-sided provider for the forwards, his presence on scoresheets would not have escaped scrutiny by the wily Chelsea manager Tommy Docherty.

Mike Milner had already staked a persuasive claim on the centre-half berth through solid and consistent performances. With only minutes left before the team lined up in the tunnel, he felt the inner strength that came from being part of a successful team. On this day, it would be tested – against arguably the best side in the land.

Hull's Chris Chilton and Ken Wagstaff were regarded by many as two of the best forwards in the entire Football League. As a strike partnership, they were deadly. Chillo was tall, powerful, fast and a brilliant header of the ball. Waggy was unselfish, deceptively quick and extraordinarily cool in front of goal. He had superb awareness and his finishing was deadly.

City manager Cliff Britton was a calm and exceptionally methodical man. Routinely, he would call for extensive dossiers on opposing teams. It was not unusual for these to be 40 pages in length. Scouts would even start their reports by describing in detail the weather conditions and scenery about the ground. No stone was left unturned.

Yet despite the attention to detail, more often than not, the Tigers would worry more about playing their own game rather than adapting to counter the opposition's style. City's strength was in their attack. They were a free-scoring side. Would the defence be good enough to win major honours?

That question was hardly on Britton's mind as the ground filled. This was the FA Cup. Anything could happen. The competition frequently brought shock results as top teams found themselves humbled on the day by motivated pretenders to the throne of cup-winning aristocrats.

At the heart of Britton's tactical philosophy was the imperative that the team must be certain of the framework in which they were operating. Creating spaces, the timing of passes and the placing of the through ball were key skills he taught. That he had the players able to execute the theory was the difference between mediocrity and success. As the magic worked, so confidence grew in the team. Riding on a wave of cup success, the Tigers were getting ever closer to the final. As Hull fans arrived at the ground, they marvelled at the magnificent stadium. This was no time for an in-depth reading the matchday programme. Nerves wouldn't allow it.

At the time, Chelsea were undoubtedly one of the top sides in the country. Star-studded and successful, their flowing style was bordering on being arrogant. Terry Venables, at age 22, had two recent full Internationals under his belt against Belgium and Holland. Formerly with Aston Villa, George Graham was 2 years younger. In 42 appearances the previous season, he'd netted 21 times.

Winger Bob Tambling had a similar tally. Peter Bonetti, John Kirkup, Eddie McCreadie, John Hollins and Marvin Hinton were all in a squad, the arts equivalent of which would have probably been Beethoven, Plato, Chaucer, Shakespeare and Michelangelo. Missing from the Chelsea line-up was an injured 18 year-old Peter Osgood. Already an England youth player, his record in front of goal was startling.

Thousands of travelling fans adorned the terraces with their amber and black rosettes, scarves and hats. As the teams took the field, their passionate cheers competed with the wall of noise from the home terraces. Waggy recalls: 'It was unbelievable walking out there. I'm not sure how many City fans were in the ground but it felt like 10,000! We saw a sea of black and amber and the fans' expectant faces. We already knew that the whole of the city of Hull was behind us. Obviously, we were up for the game for a number of reasons but the support we had in the ground really inspired us that little bit extra.'

With warm-up and pleasantries out of the way, and as the crowd roared them on, both teams faced each other. It was that special moment when expectation and reality are poised in an eerie equilibrium – broken only by a sharp blast from the referee's whistle. The game was in motion. Was this history in the making? Certainly.

In the early part of the game, the ball flowed to and fro in frenetic exchanges. Honours were even as both sides struggled for supremacy. One goal-bound shot from McCreadie cannoned against Dennis Butler and rebounded into a group of photographers nearby.

December 1965: match action as Waggy strikes for goal.

At the other end, Chris Simpkin stroked a superb long-range drive goalwards, only to be denied by Peter Bonetti who pulled the ball down from just under the bar. On the half-hour, Chelsea drew first blood. Venables stepped forward to tap a free-kick through to Tambling who, it was claimed, had just been fouled by Jock Davidson. Allegedly, the Scot had tried a second bite of the cherry as the wall lined up. Tambling had obscured his view and it was said Davidson had punched the Chelsea player in the back. He went down, but subsequent protestations to the referee fell on deaf ears. Whatever happened, Jock had no time for prima donnas. Reputations meant nothing to the tough defender.

Tambling's revenge was to unleash a powerful drive beyond Swan's reach. In that instant, the ground erupted as Chelsea fans celebrated what they felt was their just deserts. In the hearts of City fans there were mixed emotions. One down, but certainly not out, they knew what their side were capable of doing. In reassurance, they saw the determined body language of the players. They were still in there with a chance.

Later in the first half, the Tigers clearly should have had a penalty. Chilton broke down the right-hand side and crossed the ball from the byline. Houghton headed in powerfully towards goal as the black-and-amber faithful held their breath. In desperation, a Chelsea player cleared the ball off the line with his hand.

Waggy had a clear view of the incident. With total clarity he recalls: 'It was a definite penalty. Everyone in the crowd knew it was a penalty. The defender punched it off the line with his hand! We were ripped off.' It was a desperate blow.

Sixth-round cup drama at Stamford Bridge on 26 March 1966. City's Maurice Swan turns a McReadie shot on to the angle of the crossbar.

Skipper Andy Davidson was furious at the referee's decision. As the teams walked off at half time, he spoke to the offending player who he claims replied simply: 'What would you have done?' The incident still rankles years after the event. Davidson is adamant that everyone in the ground knew it was a penalty. As referee Jack Taylor waved play on, it seemed a great injustice had been done.

The following Saturday, Taylor again refereed Hull City's game at Oxford United. City won the match 2-0 with goals from Houghton and Wagstaff. To this day, Waggy is adamant that both goals in that game should have been disallowed. Without the slightest doubt in his voice he affirmed: 'I was at least 10 yards offside.' Later in the game, the referee ignored him when he asked pointedly: 'Is that for last week at Chelsea?' Taylor just walked away.

Andy Davidson recalls the Oxford game: 'We were diabolical at Oxford. In the goals he let us get away with, it seemed he was trying to make up for the Chelsea decision. As we walked off he said: "That was better, wasn't it?" Ron Atkinson was captain of Oxford at the time. After the game, he said to me: "You were lucky today Andy. Was that your dad refereeing?"'

The Taylor decision at Stamford Bridge had left the Tigers with a job still to do. Unfortunately, the task became an even greater burden as the first half wore on. Four minutes from the interval, Chelsea went two ahead. Having forced a corner, Tambling directed his cross to the head of George Graham who managed to out-climb the Hull defenders.

For Chelsea manager Tommy Docherty and the jubilant supporters it was simply how they'd expected things to pass. After all, they were the aristocrats of the Football League and Hull were the underdogs by two divisions. It seemed that the Tigers needed a miracle. At the very least, they needed a player to turn the game. They had such players.

According to Ken Wagstaff, although Chelsea were in front, the Tigers were still confident: 'Although we were 2-0 down, we didn't change our game. We knew we'd score because they were very lax at the back. They hadn't done their homework thoroughly on us. The manager just told us to go out and play our game and that's exactly what we did. At half time when we were two down, we were still confident. There was no better winger than Ian Butler and no better forward than Chris Chilton. As a team we could play and that gave us the confidence.'

Mick Brown, who learned his trade with the Tigers and who went on to take up several prestigious coaching and scouting appointments (most recently with Manchester United as Chief Scout), was the 12th man for that game. In the dressing room at half-time, he recalls skipper Andy Davidson being upset at the way things had gone. Despite the fact the Tigers were playing well, he'd felt decisions had wrongly gone against them. 'Andy Davidson was extremely unhappy at half time,' says Mick. 'He was totally committed to the cause – a very passionate player. Despite the pressure on the forwards, the calmest man in the dressing room was Waggy. He just said quietly: 'Just tell him to get the ball up to me.' It wasn't the first time Waggy's words had been prophetic. Things often seemed to happen just as he'd predicted.

Hull manager Cliff Britton had seen Doc's complacency as a fatal weakness. He knew that he had the talent to match Chelsea. With a little luck, he felt they could win the game. The second half continued, with Hull fans becoming concerned that, with every passing minute, their chances of progress were receding. Yet, out there on the pitch were two forwards in whom they had every confidence – Chillo and Waggy. Still, as the clock ticked ever closer to the final whistle, nerves were increasingly on edge.

With ten minutes of the match left, hearts were sinking among the black-and-amber faithful. The home terraces were triumphant. In Waggy's local at Willerby, the regulars were glued to the TV news reports. Some were starting to drown their sorrows. Yet, they were reasonably pleased with the reported performance of their heroes. They had made superb progress in the competition so far. The team had acquitted themselves well on the day. It was no debacle. City fans everywhere shared that view. Yet, they remained anxious for news. Would a miracle happen?

At the ground, Tommy Docherty's body language was revealing. Relaxed and looking supremely confident of victory, it seemed Chelsea had the tie under their belt. Having seen Hull turn out a below-par performance two weeks earlier, Doc's smug smile on leaving the Boothferry Park had said it all.

Later, he'd seen a better performance at Reading but the complacency on the big day was there for all to see. Things were working out pretty much as he'd expected. His thoughts turned to the final whistle, which was now only minutes away. Surely this game was in the bag? In the press box, journalists were phoning copy through to their editors. For some, deadlines for the evening papers were minutes away. Very soon, the headlines would be inserted and the presses would roll.

Hull continued to battle, in a match that has seen them deserve greater reward for their considerable efforts. Victory would make them only the fifth Division Three side to reach the semi-finals. Fifty-one years earlier Chelsea had hammered the Tigers 5-1. Were they again dead and buried? Time would tell, and it was running out fast.

In the 80th minute, characteristic trickery by Ian Butler on the left wing led to a cross that flew across the Chelsea area. The gist of what happened next has been re-lived by Hull fans again and again over subsequent years. Slow-motion video shows the sequence of events. As Chris Chilton raced goalwards to the left, Waggy ghosted towards the far post. He'd sensed the trajectory of Butler's cross with an awesome telepathy and his measured run was timed to perfection.

With the Chelsea defence caught like rabbits in a car's headlights, his right foot met the ball. With the lightest of touches he steered it into the right corner of the goal. The accuracy was unerring and the effect of his action devastating. The Chelsea fans fell silent.

Suddenly, the tie looked anything but settled. The Hull striker had, yet again, made it look simple. Such is the hallmark of a quality forward. Despite the enormity of the occasion, the lateness of the moment and the sheer weight of responsibility, he was in the right place at the right time with an unerring finish. In an instant, the game was transformed.

The scene was set for a frantic drama as both sides battled for possession. This was a David-versus-Goliath contest and the Division One giants were now on the rack. Although it was a Hull team effort, only another inspired City strike would rescue the situation. All hopes were pinned on the two forwards to deliver that all-important goal.

Eternally elusive, and with surprising pace for his stocky build, Waggy's unselfish and intelligent play was complimented by deadly finishing. He was the ultimate goal-poacher at close range but was equally capable of scoring from longer distances. Being in the right place at the right time was taken to an art form. His style was certainly different – but the ability to do something unexpected made him great.

As the clock ticked on, Wagstaff drifted into free spaces with the commanding strides of Chilton ever threatening. With only two minutes of the game left, City won a free kick just inside their own half. From a Dennis Butler kick, the ball arced into the Chelsea half and cannoned off a defender on to the back of Waggy's head as he raced forward – the ball now at his feet.

Hull City and Mansfield player David Coates is clear about Wagstaff's sublime talent: 'As a player, Waggy was razor sharp. Nobody I knew could have turned that quick.' In characteristic style, he ghosted past McReadie and Kirkup as panic spread throughout the Chelsea rearguard. Now, one on one with the 'keeper, the striker coolly rounded the fabled Bonetti and struck the ball home. As it hit the back of the net, the amber-and-black army erupted as hope replaced despondency.

In the Springhead pub at Willerby, they were dancing on the tables. Across the city, fans began celebrating. That this action took place in the space of a split second is at the heart of the immense talent. No nerves, no hesitation and no hanging around. The Tigers were level! Skipper Andy Davidson recalls: 'It seemed like an eternity before Waggy finally released his shot. Most other players would have blasted it and risked hitting the defenders. He didn't shoot until he was certain the defenders were beaten and the goalkeeper was at his mercy. It was exceptional skill and coolness – executed in a flash.'

Speed, awareness, positioning sense, coolness and shooting skill came together in the blink of an eye to turn the game. That such traits demonstrated repeatedly were part of the raw talent that made Ken Wagstaff great. It was Hull's 100th goal of the season. The brilliantly executed strike silenced the home fans.

With Chelsea's morale now destroyed, the rampant Tigers moved in for the kill. With only seconds remaining, an anxious Docherty eyed his watch. For him, there was still time for disaster to strike. His furrowed expression told the story eloquently. Barked orders to his back-pedalling thoroughbreds went unheeded as Hull's Alan Jarvis sighted for a last-ditch shot on goal. The Welshman struck the ball powerfully and accurately. His 'exocet' released, it took only milliseconds for the crowd to realise that the trajectory was threatening. In those final moments of truth, thousands of adrenaline-pumping fans held their breath as the strike homed in at breathtaking speed.

With only feet left before impact, Bonetti was beaten. Now, just inches away, the ball appeared destined for the back of the net. The thump of leather on wood went unheard. Yet, the sight of an empty goal brought forth a blast of emotion. As the ball skidded into the stand, a wave of contradictory feelings were released – both relief and disappointment pulsing simultaneously into the ether.

The ball had shaved the bar and ricocheted safely away. Chelsea could breathe again. Certainly, they had survived by virtue of their skill, but on the day it was also in large measure due to good fortune and erroneous refereeing. As the final whistle blew, Hull left the field triumphant. They had taken on the elite Chelsea, gone two behind, drawn level and finally had the Londoners on the rack. Whatever happened next, it was an historic day. After the match, a clearly delighted Cliff Britton congratulated the team on their brilliant performance. It had been classic game that would be talked about for years and form part of the club's folklore. In the imposing cauldron that was Stamford Bridge on that day, at a time when the Tigers were almost dead and buried, yet again Ken Wagstaff complemented the play and skills of colleagues with individual brilliance and ice-cool finishing. He was toasted in pubs and bars across the city that evening. It was yet another page written in the book of golden memories that will live forever in the hearts of Hull City fans.

The Chelsea cup tie was a major landmark in the long history of the club. In such situations and in such moments, it is possible to discover the essence of what football means for those who follow the game. Of those who perform on the pitch, there are also insights into what makes them tick. It is often possible to see their true character and to witness those skills that make them great.

Of course, the team as a whole deserved the greatest credit for their exceptional feat. While there were several other individual performances worthy of note on that day, Stamford Bridge was one major arena in which Waggy's temperament and exceptional talent were dramatically displayed for the football world to see. Cometh the hour: cometh the man. He was a dedicated footballer who was totally focussed – a man with no major personal ambitions outside the game. An admirer of the great Denis Law, his favourite team at the time was Manchester United. For him their exciting, inspired team play and the individual brilliance of key players epitomised his view of how the game should be played.

In a sparkling career filled with excitement and achievement, the Chelsea FA Cup tie is perhaps his greatest football memory. In turn, his performance encapsulated all his personal and football qualities in the space of that 90 minutes. Although he loved steak and the occasional lager, scoring was his real meat and drink. It was his driving force – the ultimate professional objective. However, that didn't stop him from playing the team game and creating goal after goal for colleagues.

Joe Eaton, the long-serving secretary of Waggy's former club Mansfield Town describes him as 'the complete player – a real goal-getter.' Waggy's performance at Chelsea came as no surprise to his admirers – either in Mansfield or in Hull. His coolness, determination and unerring eye for goal was his trademark. He was equally deadly throughout any game – from the first minute to the last. In match after match his influence was decisive – either in laying on chances for colleagues or by taking them himself. Yet, the importance of having quality players alongside was always important.

Brought into the Mansfield team aged seventeen by Raich Carter, he quickly delivered the promise that had earned him a reputation in the Nottingham minor leagues. In the space of a few seasons, his goalscoring feats attracted the attention of several top Division One clubs. However, it was ambitious Division Three Hull City that secured his services. At Boothferry Park, Cliff Britton relied on the well-proven formula of combining experience and youth on a solid defensive foundation. Combining the attacking talents of Wagstaff, Chilton, Butler and Houghton was a masterstroke.

Heroes' homecoming: Hull City players pictured arriving back at Paragon Station, Hull, from King's Cross after the FA Cup tie against Chelsea at Stamford Bridge on 26 March 1966.

Waggy never underestimated the opposition. For him, they were all treated with the greatest respect. His ambition was to play in Division One. Early in his League career, he helped Mansfield win promotion from Division Three. Within two seasons of joining Hull City, he was playing in Division Two. For a while, the club were on the verge of a promotion place.

Management's failure to strengthen the defence at that key phase in the team's development has been cited by observers as the reason why Division One ambitions were not realised. Indeed, it is a consensus view that, had Waggy played for a more fashionable team at a higher level, International honours would have inevitable followed. Yet he remained loyal and continued to score goals with alacrity throughout the 1960s and indeed until his left the club as a result of accumulated injuries in 1975.

On the occasion of their centenary, the Football League conducted a poll of all clubs to find out who was the most popular player in the history of each club. Ken Wagstaff

In front of a packed and cheering Field Mill in 2001, former Mansfield Town player and long-serving club secretary Joe Eaton, presents Ken Wagstaff with the silver salver award for the Stags' all-time most popular player.

topped the poll for both his former clubs – Mansfield Town and Hull City. He was the only player to win the dual accolade.

As a footballer, his record is outstanding. He has a deserving place as an all-time great in the hearts of those who were privileged to witness his football magic. His personal qualities were also worthy of note. He was dedicated, loyal, focussed and determined.

The story starts in Langwith on 24 November 1942.

2

The Early Years

On the day Ken Wagstaff was born, the Nottinghamshire mining village of Langwith was destined for a place on the football map of Great Britain – thanks to the new resident at 45 Church Street. It was wartime Britain. The sound of air-raid sirens and the throb of Heinkel bomber engines had brought terror to major cities, docklands and industrial areas.

As Vera Lynn first sang 'White Cliffs of Dover', Spitfire pilots duelled high above the fields and villages of southern England. Watched by thousands below, they carved their name in history. As the sun went down on 24 November 1942, a new hero had been born in this land. In post-war Britain, football would become the peaceful battlefield upon which Ken Wagstaff and many of his contemporaries would fight for sporting supremacy in front of great audiences.

Oblivious to their son's future fame, Clarice and George brought up their family through hard times. The outbreak of war had seen Ken's father take a job in the local coal mine. While some saw this as a smart move, the reality was that hazards under-

Ken's father George and his mother Clarice brought their children up through hard times.

ground often made the job more perilous than the front line. George didn't enjoy the best of health and that placed further strains on the family economy. Large families were not uncommon, but the eventual arrival of Terry, Derek and Marlene added significantly to the burdens. Yet, the Wagstaff household was happy, if not rich.

With the war over, a new mood of optimism in the country was conceived on promises of a better life. Yet it was business as usual at the coalface. In the village, adults visited the pub, raced pigeons and read newspapers. On Saturdays, many villagers would travel to either Mansfield or Rotherham to watch the professional football teams play. Some watched amateur and youth games in the nearby playing fields. Although it would not be long before Ken Wagstaff would learn his trade on those grounds, he cut his teeth as a 5-year-old on the narrow streets outside his home.

As soon as it was considered safe for him to be outside unsupervised, young Ken began playing football with the two Nettle brothers who lived a few doors away. That there were no broken windows or resounding crashes from a bouncing ball was more a reflection of the family finances, rather than disciplined consideration for residents. In fact, hardly anyone had enough money to buy a football in those days.

Ken relied on his sister Marlene to provide parts from an old teddy bear. On weekdays, they would use the bear's arms and legs. Fifty-five years on and with that inimitable cheeky smirk Ken still recalls that: 'We used to save the bear's head for the final on Sundays.' Oblivious to Ken's antics as a kid, Tigers fans in the 1960s bought their children teddy bears and called them Waggy!

The youngsters would play for hours in the narrow street outside Ken's house. They used the gateways of opposite houses as goalmouths as Waggy learned his trade by

Langwith Imps. Ken Wagstaff is pictured second from right, middle row.

beating the brothers and calmly driving the 'ball' up the opposition's pathway. This was no sports centre or five-a-side hall with the dubious luxury of a one-two with the wall. The Langwith Back Street Academy of Football taught Waggy the one-on-one skills of how to beat an opponent and score. It was basic: but it proved effective.

Thousands of miles away in Brazil, hard-up kids would make similar improvisations. Some would go on to become World Championship-winning footballers, their early experiences preparing them well for that task. And in the streets of Newcastle and other hotbeds of soccer, other poor kids were also preparing to become heroes. In time, they would drive expensive sports cars and be fashion icons. For now, it was simply for the love of the game.

Eventually, the long happy days in Church Street came to an end. It was time for young Wagstaff to start school. Like all the other mums Clarice would wait outside the school gates for her little darling. Already a 22-carat so-and-so, he would almost invariably do the opposite to what he was asked. And so it was one day when mum waved him to leave the school at one particular side of the gate, Waggy emerged at speed from the other side! Years later, he would continue the mischief by sending goalkeepers and defenders the wrong way.

As time went by, the irrepressible youngster was given a small tennis ball by his grandfather. Later he set his sights on a proper football and hit on a master plan. He'd observed neighbours giving the rag-and-bone man various objects in return for cash. One day, he saw a small quantity of lead change hands for a tidy sum. The next evening he scaled a drainpipe at the school just a little further down the road and removed a fairly small amount of lead from the roof, thinking that it wouldn't be missed.

Some might see Ken's act as simply a wise, though unknowing, investment by the Education Authority in his career. Unfortunately, the police viewed it rather differently and the little entrepreneur found himself in court and on probation. The offence was discovered when rain fell on teachers and pupils during assembly. It is difficult to know how the culprit was actually traced but it could well have connected to the fact that Ken was one of the few kids in the village able to afford a proper football!

At Whaley Thornes junior school, his attendance record was abysmal. He rarely turned up – preferring to run along to his grandfather's allotment where he would pass the time looking after the pigeons that were kept in a shed. Ever a surprise, he put the knowledge gained to good use by writing an award-winning essay on the birds for his sister.

Granddad did his best to encourage Ken's football mania. Eventually, he bought him a pair of football boots. Aged about seven at the time, Ken was playing for a school team. He recalls that: 'Granddad bought me this pair of football boots. They were great. I was thrilled to bits and scored several goals in my first game wearing them. After the match, he pointed out that I'd got them on the wrong feet! There was some degree of inevitability about Ken's talent such that granddad predicted that one day he would be on television.

At home, the young boy was a constant mischief. On one occasion, mum caught him disobeying instructions not to take more bread and jam from the kitchen. Grabbing the bread knife she swiftly tapped him on the head. Unfortunately, by mistake, she had used the blade end. The wound needed several stitches and Ken still has the scar as a memory of what in hindsight was a funny incident!

Despite the lack of regular instruction, Waggy was a bright lad and learned enough on his rare appearances at school to enable him to finish in the top half of the class. A keen athlete, he won most events he was entered for on sports day. In particular, he excelled at running and long jump, where he demonstrated extremely good balance. It was hardly surprising that frequent absences from class often led to him being lined up for the 'high jump' as well!

'Dad was a real character when he was alive,' Waggy remembered. 'Once he had a go at me when I tripped and let a kid called Tiger Wall beat me in a race. Although I made up for it next time round, he was a bit shirty about the earlier slip up. He must have had a bet or something with the other kid's dad!'

Mum was always receiving calls from the headmaster about her son's absences. On arrival at home she would question him, knowing full well he'd have been kicking a ball around somewhere, or messing around at the allotment. Soon, the young Wagstaff became familiar with the phrase – 'You've not been at school again, have you? You little bleeder.'

The teachers soon resigned themselves to the boy's ways. Their tolerance may well have been attributable to a desire for harmony with the star forward who was scoring goal after goal for the school football team. When he was needed for a game, the PE teacher would dispatch two pupils to the allotment with the instruction: 'Go and tell Waggy there's a match.' Those words were enough to guarantee an appearance. Even at this early age, all he wanted to do was play football. There were no other interests. It was in his blood. Scoring goals was almost an obsession. It was, by now, almost second nature. In junior football he went on to score around 200 goals!

Just before Waggy reached the age of 10, the Wagstaffs moved house to Shirebrook. Waggy continued missing school. It was about seven months before the truancy was detected. Both his old and his new school were under the impression he was attending the other school.

By the time he was 11, Ken was helping to deliver coal. At that time the fuel was tipped from the back of a lorry, but by the time he was 14, it was being delivered in bags. He would handle up to 30 tons every day. There is little doubt that the upper-body strength and power that came from humping those sacks of coal in his youth served Waggy well when later he would have to contend with burly defenders at his shoulder!

Although Ken's academic youth was hardly exemplary, he still managed to finish in the top six. It's difficult to predict what he might have achieved given an improved attendance. Yet, his ambition was to be a footballer. Maths and geography were a secondary consideration. He explains in his usual straightforward style: 'Despite hardly ever turning up, I was quite a brainy kid at school. Well I wasn't thick. This was a mining area. People couldn't imagine any career other than the pit. Football, cricket, racing pigeons and the pub were the main form of entertainment. I wanted to be a footballer. Exams didn't interest me.'

In those early teen years, Ken continued to play for school sides. It was in these games that he would first meet up with opposition players who would later be team-mates in the senior local league teams. Immediately after leaving school Ken followed in his dad's footsteps and went down the local mine for around 9 months. He is clear about the learning value of working in a pit: 'Going down the mine taught me a great deal. It taught me to get out!'

It was a hard life. Long hours, dirty working conditions and strenuous work were the order of the day. Danger was never far away. At weekends he would play football for a pit team formed by two of the employees – Geoff Briggs and Ron Elliot. The Woodland Imps played in a local league and Waggy became their centre forward.

Eventually, the manager of the mine saw him play and promoted him to the pit's senior team. Langwith Miners Welfare played in a tough league with top-notch amateur sides – including the likes of Heanor Town and Shirebrook Miners Welfare. Effectively, the 15 year old found himself playing against grown men 10 years his senior.

Shortly afterwards, and now a mere 16 years old, Ken left home and joined the

Langwith Imps – Ken Wagstaff, aged 11.

groundstaff at Rotherham United football club. In the mornings he'd swill out the toilets, sweep round and clean boots for the senior team players. Training followed in the afternoons and on Saturday there'd be a game for the 'A' team. Although he couldn't have known it at the time, Waggy would eventually team up with many of his contemporaries who were playing and living in the Rotherham area. Ian Butler and Ken Houghton were two great players in that category. Waggy recalls: 'Frank Casper was there at the time. I remember first meeting Ian Butler at Rotherham. We both played together in a match for England Schoolboys at Sunderland at that time.' Ken Houghton also came from Rotherham.

Ian Butler recalls his days as a junior at Rotherham United and his friendship with Ken Wagstaff. In addition to recognizing Waggy's football talent, he also became aware of the family humour: 'Ken was scoring goals even in those early days. However, he was a poor timekeeper at that time – rolling up late for training. The manager wasn't too pleased about it. Once, I went to Waggy's home in Langwith. As I was waiting for him to get ready, his dad was pulling on some pit boots before going to work. Suddenly, his wife said: "You're putting them boots on the wrong feet." Quick as a flash, he replied:

Ken Wagstaff at a sports dinner in 1992 with the man who discovered him and set him on the road to stardom, Raich Carter.

"You're right love. They should be on yours." Waggy was no different with his wit and he didn't know it. We'd be rolling about laughing at what he'd said and then we'd have to explain to him why it was so funny!'

After 8 months of being unsettled on the groundstaff, things finally came to a head. Waggy explained things to his father who listened sympathetically: 'I didn't like living in digs away from home at the time. It just didn't feel right. In the mornings I'd go in and clean the boots of first team players and then swill out the toilets, polish seats and a load of other jobs about the ground. Then, in the afternoon it was training. We'd play a game on Saturday for the 'A' team. The crunch came one day when we were due to go and play at Heckmondwike. I told dad that I didn't want to go.'

Dad's advice to Ken was to follow his instinct and to avoid what made him unhappy. For Waggy, football was great, but Rotherham was not for him. He returned home, much to the annoyance of manager Tom Johnson who was reported to have said: 'Fancy that. He's just buggered off – and I've just paid for his haircut!'

On his return home, Ken returned to play for Woodland Imps again. Clearly, it was a successful homecoming because the team went on to win the local league and cup competitions. The final was to be more than memorable because of the result. It marked a major change in fortunes thanks to a man who was a football legend in his own lifetime, Raich Carter.

Joe Eaton was the secretary of Mansfield Town Football Club at the time. A former part-time professional with the club, he was the product of Langwith Boys Club, as were Ken Wagstaff and Ray Wilson of Everton and England fame. He made his debut against Crewe in November 1952 and a year later was appointed assistant secretary, taking over a year later as secretary. At the time, Joe was an employee of Mansfield Brewery. The brewer's boss was also chairman of the football club and when difficulties arose in filling the administrative post, Joe was drafted in to solve the problem.

After a couple of years, the Football League decreed that it was not possible to carry out both functions at the same time. Only 25 years of age, Joe became the youngest club secretary in the League and occupied the post for a further 25 years. Initially, Joe served with team manager Charlie Mitten, the ex-Manchester United player. Mitten had gone on to become player-manager with Fulham before being appointed at Field Mill. Two years later, Sam Weaver took over the reins but was himself replaced by the great Raich Carter in February 1960. Carter was destined to play a decisive role in the course of Ken Wagstaff's football career.

The silver-haired maestro, who played for his country at age 20, became a hero at Sunderland and led them to the League Championship in 1936/37. He scored one of the goals in the 3-1 FA Cup final victory in 1937. After the war, Carter moved to Derby County and took them to their first-ever FA Cup win. Uniquely, he'd won FA Cup winners' medal both prior to and after the war.

In March 1948, he moved to Hull City in the combined role of player and assistant manager to Frank Buckley. His debut came late in the season and Hull finished fifth in Division Three North. In the next term, the Tigers roared along a record-breaking, championship-winning path to the best season in their entire history. Unbeaten in their first 11 games, Carter brought Don Revie into the side as Boothferry Park swelled with the crowds scenting a possibility of Division One football at long last.

Unfortunately, off-the-field events conspired to cause Carter to resign as player-manager. The club's fortunes dipped dramatically and but for his return shortly after as a player, the club could well have been relegated. It was his last season at Hull. He went on to manage Leeds United before moving to take over the helm at Mansfield Town.

With heavy irony, he would discover and develop Ken Wagstaff and years later finish second to his protégé as the most popular Hull City player of all time – an accolade that Waggy also won for his feats at Mansfield Town. The architect of his own failure to attain the Hull City award, Carter's moment of doom came on a football pitch in Shirebrook on a Friday evening in spring 1960.

Joe Eaton recalls the lead up to the now-famous discovery: 'Raich came into the office one day and asked me if I knew where to find the Shirebrook football ground. He said that he wanted to look at a centre forward in a youth cup final taking place that Friday evening. In fact it wasn't Waggy that he wanted to see. There had been a lot of publicity in the press about another player. At the game, Langwith got a penalty and Waggy missed it. Nonetheless Raich had seen something in Ken's play that appealed to him. 'He asked me to get permission from the club officials to speak to him. In a meeting with Waggy after the game, Raich complimented him on his performance and asked him if he wanted to be a professional footballer. When he'd got the answer he wanted, Raich invited Ken along to the ground for discussions on the following Monday. He came with his father. Waggy then joined us for pre-season training and was signed as a player – for £50!'

Ken recalls: 'I remember that game because I missed two penalties. We won 3-1 in the end. At the end of the match, I remember Raich Carter coming over to talk to me. I hadn't known he was there. Dad just came up with him. His first words were: "I'd like a word with you boy. How would you like to come and play for Mansfield Town?" Dad was okay with it and so I went along.'

At last, Ken had achieved his ambition to become a professional footballer. From back-street ball player to full-time professional had taken but a few formative years. He was still a youngster, yet his talent was to be recognised not with spells in the juniors and reserves but with a baptism of fire straight into the first team. He was well prepared. By most standards he wasn't old enough – but was he good enough?

3

Rising Star 1960–62

Now a professional footballer, about to be thrown into the deep end, the 17-year-old Ken Wagstaff was better prepared than most for sudden introduction to the hurly burly of life in the lower divisions of the Football League. He had a natural talent, a high level of fitness, great energy, a solid frame and great upper-body strength. But he was destined to live away from home and the influence of his grandmother, who had kept a close eye on him in recent years.

With great foresight, the club ensured that Ken was always in suitable digs and under appropriate influences. With a little more imagination, they might easily have envisaged that the cheeky youngster would sidestep the master plan, dodge round the impediments, remould the shape of barriers and continue with his social agenda in his own sweet way.

Former Hull City player David Coates was transferred to Mansfield Town in March 1960. With a few months under his belt as a Stags player, he recalls first seeing the newly

Mansfield Town. From left to right, back row: Sid Carter, Sammy Chapman, Colin Toon, Peter Morris, Colin Treherne, John Gill, Mick Jones, Wilf Humble, Tommy Cummings. Front row: Brian Hall, Colin Askey, David Coates, Ken Wagstaff, Ivan Hollitt, Albert Scanlon, Roy Chapman.

Raich Carter, Ken Wagstaff, Brian Phillips and Brian Tarrant in 1960.

recruited Ken Wagstaff at pre-season training. In fact Waggy trained only for a matter of days before disappearing from the scene for a week. Having been given a dispensation by Raich Carter 'The Wag', as some of his Stags team-mates called him, had gone on a pre-booked Miners' Welfare Club holiday to Skegness!

David recalls having a go at the young upstart on his return to the fold: 'I told Wag that while he'd been away, we'd all been going up hill and down dale sweating our way to fitness. He was completely unphased by what I'd said. Instead he chuckled and told me that it was no problem because he was already fit and that it was me that needed the extra training! That was typical Ken. He was a real joker. Raich Carter once told me that the whole story was in his name. He was a real Wag and full of confidence!'

There were many other examples throughout Ken's career of how that cheeky manner was reflected in his play. In pre-season training at Mansfield, David recalls a further amazing incident involving Waggy and big Brian Phillips: 'We were pre-season training and Ken was the new boy – just a youngster among hardened professionals. There was a practice game on between reserves and the first team. The Wag was centre forward for the reserves. He'd dribbled the ball through to the edge of the box and was met with big strapping centre half, Brian Phillips. Brian didn't suffer fools gladly. He was built like a tree trunk, a leader of men – forward into battle! Ken did what he did thousands of times to defenders through his career. He went one way to shoot, but dummied. By then Brian had stuck his foot out and committed himself totally. "Unlucky!" cried Waggy who then took it over on to his other foot. The defender then tried to counter it and lost it. "Unlucky again!" Waggy then took it over to his other foot and lashed a drive against the foot of the post with the skipper looking a complete Charlie. To add insult to injury, Ken chuckled at him triumphantly. Brian Phillips was livid and threatened to kick his arse. The Wag trotted off chuckling: "You'll have to catch me first!"'

Although nobody got away with making a monkey out of the centre half, Phillips actually had a great affection for the youngster. Although not everyone in the future would be so generous, Brian understood Waggy's brand of humour, liked the cheek and respected the abundant football skills being displayed. In fact, that view was one shared by the vast majority of players at Mansfield Town Football Club.

One day, while driving away from Field Mill with husband Raich, Pat Carter recalls him pointing out Wagstaff among a bunch of players walking out of the ground. He said: 'You see that boy there. He will be a great player. If he gets with the right club, he should play for England one day.'

As time went by, Waggy would endear himself more and more, not only to his team-mates but also to the football-mad fans at Field Mill. Ken recalls his early days as a Mansfield Town player: 'In those days, I used to go to the ground on a bus with my football boots in a supermarket bag.' Fellow player David Coates remembers that: 'Waggy used to just arrive and get changed in the space of five minutes maximum. Some of the other players would take ages. He just got on with it. It was no different on the field.'

The season started badly for the Stags with a 2-0 away defeat at Aldershot. At home to Rochdale two days later, they lost by the same margin. There was some improvement in the following game with honours even in a four-goal contest. On 30 August, together with Peter Morris and Michael Stringfellow, Ken Wagstaff made his Football League debut at Rochdale in front of 5,547 Dale fans. Stringfellow was a fast natural winger. He could go past defenders with ease and provide perfect crosses. It wasn't rocket science, but Carter's chemistry experiment would in due course become explosive in goalscoring terms.

Waggy celebrated his first game in grand style, reversing the earlier result at Field Mill and scoring both goals himself. He had arrived. Although, he was not yet to be seen on TV screens, his grandfather's prophecy had all but come true. Unfortunately, the old man had not lived long enough to witness the event – having passed away two years earlier.

In a carefully planned strategy of introducing youth to the side, manager Raich Carter was slowly slotting into place the pieces of a colourful promotion jigsaw. It would be another season before the scene became completely clear. For now, Ken contented himself with gaining League experience and settling into the side. By the time New Year bells rang, he'd netted four times, in spite of the fact that he was not playing in a central role. He was in no doubt about the wisdom of Raich's daring strategy: 'Raich dramatically introduced youth to the side. As 17-year-olds, we went straight into the first team. I didn't play any games in the reserves. It was in-at-the-deep-end stuff. Raich always said: "If a player is good enough, then he's old enough." The team had not been doing very well. He was right to try it. Mike Stringfellow was a fast brilliant winger. Then he introduced Peter Morris. We were all 17 at the time. There were other players in there as well. Brian Phillips, Sammy Chapman and Roy Chapman were all very good players. Davis Coates was an excellent athlete who could run all day for us. Raich put together a very talented side.'

On 24 February 1961, in an away game at Workington, Carter laid a further key piece in his jigsaw in the shape of Peter Morris playing his debut. The Stags won 3-1 in a manner that gave Carter great satisfaction. David Coates recalls the coach trip back to Mansfield: 'After that match, we saw a little-known side of Raich Carter. Having won the game, one of the players asked Raich if we could have a drink on the way back. To our great surprise, he agreed. We stopped off at a pub somewhere and the lads duly got a round in. We couldn't see the manager in the bar and before long the boys were having another. After the third, I remember going to the toilet. Through a slightly open snug door, I saw the great Raich Carter with a crowd of locals. Obviously, a different man after a couple of sherries, they were laughing at his jokes and hanging on to his every word as he reminisced about his playing days.'

On the back of the Workington game, the Stags repeated the scoreline at home against Chester. They added a further victory away to Chester a week later. Mansfield played Accrington Stanley twice in successive games during March that year. The home leg ended in a goal-less draw, but three days later, Accrington were turned over 4-1 – with Wagstaff scoring twice. The team were now forming a much closer understanding and confidence was growing by the game.

Unfortunately, Oldham Athletic bucked the trend and inflicted two defeats on the Stags in the space of four days, ending on 3 April. In fact, sandwiched between those reversals of fortune was an April Fool's Day clash at Field Mill against Millwall. The Stags won that game 5-1 – with Stringfellow emulating David Coates's tally that day by scoring twice.

With the exception of a 1-0 home win against Gillingham, the Stags suffered three defeats by 2-1 scorelines – with Bradford Park Avenue doing the double over them. The side was languishing at the foot of Division Four with the spectre of re-election out of the League looming large. However, the final three games of the season, offered some hope, with two victories and a goal-less draw.

Through the gloom of inconsistency, shone several bright rays of light. In the last 11 League games of the season, Wagstaff had scored five goals. His partner in crime, Michael Stringfellow, had scored only one less. They were starting to gel. In his first season, Waggy played 27 games, almost all on the right wing, and scored 9 times. Mansfield escaped the ignominy of re-election in the last game of the season.

Club secretary Joe Eaton recalls Carter saying earlier in the season that the introduction of the youngsters would take the Stags forward: 'Raich came into the office one day and said to me: "It does me the power of good watching those boys training. They are the future of the club. They will do it for us." He often spent time himself talking to them and coaching them after the older players had gone. Raich had a lot of time for the youngsters.'

The policy was starting to work but time was needed to forge teamwork and to understand how best to deploy the emerging talent in a tactical sense – and in a way that got the best from the aptitudes of the individual players.

Raich Carter was by now fixed on the strategy of keeping youth in the attack. However, Waggy's role in the forward line was about to change dramatically and he would adopt a more central position partnered by the burly ball winner Roy Chapman. He would become the perfect foil for Waggy's talent. Michael Stringfellow had been a sensation at outside left and would continue his magic in that position.

The 1961/62 season started deceptively with a 3-1 win at home to Exeter. Although the gate at Field Mill rose to more than 9,000, hopes of a new dawn were dimmed a little after 1-0 setback against Barrow. The 5-0 debacle at Wrexham in the next game was enough to start tongues wagging. Could Carter cut it in Division Four? Certainly, he had complete support from the players, many of which had great respect for the great man's record as a player.

In the next six games, Town went unbeaten with four victories – all of

Joe Eaton, former player and secretary of Mansfield Town, pictured in 2002.

which demonstrated the considerable firepower of the forwards. The manager's emphasis on youth in the front line was at least starting to pay some dividend as attendances at Field Mill swelled to more than 10,000.

Stringfellow, Chapman and Wagstaff all found the net during that wonderful spell in September. The developing partnership between Wagstaff and Chapman was two-way, with both players feeding off each other and finding the net repeatedly.

For the Stags, unpredictability was becoming alarmingly predictable. October was dour. A six-game spell brought four defeats. In the next half-dozen games in the run up to Christmas the win–lose balance was even. The fans were unimpressed with the team's performances and League position. Gates were drifting downwards again.

On 11 November the Stags played Chester at home. It was a close game – settled by a Wagstaff opportunist strike. In a period of frenetic activity in the Chester goal area the ball was struck hard against the post. It rebounded out into a mêlée of players. David Coates was on the spot: 'We were desperately looking for the winner. The ball hit the Chester post. Everyone was ball watching as it flashed back out again. Everyone that is, except Waggy. He just followed through and lashed it into the net. On the way back for the re-start, I said to him: "Lucky bastard." He replied: "No Dave son. That's not luck.

Cartoon in *Mansfield Press*. Raich Carter's youth policy.

You've got to read the game." I mean, I was seven years older than him and he kept calling me son! But I didn't mind. He was cocky all right – but he was genuinely loved and admired by his colleagues. Prolific scorers always follow the shot. They are always on the move. Waggy always seemed to be in the right place at the right time.'

Two defeats in a row prior to Christmas certainly had an effect on the Boxing Day attendance for the game against Rochdale, when just over 6,000 rolled up on a day when gates should have been inflated by fans in holiday spirit.

In fact, 'spirits' were fast becoming a hot topic. Although Carter was a strict disciplinarian, he appeared to turn a blind eye to Waggy's reported liking of a pint at various local hostelries. David Coates had a good insight into what was happening at the time: 'The Wag liked a drink. Raich turned a blind eye to it at first – especially since the lad always trained hard and was very fit. It never stopped him scoring goals. However, drinking before a match was strictly not acceptable.'

On Christmas night 1961, just hours before he was due to play in the game against Rochdale, Ken Wagstaff and two other Mansfield players were having a 'quiet drink' in Mansfield's town centre. Although there was some speculation later by fans that he'd been 'as quiet as a newt', the reality was that the players had simply decided to round the evening off with a visit to the local dance hall. Unfortunately, the doormen had other ideas and refused them entry. Although there was no question of drunken behaviour, the interchange between the players and the bouncers was such that police had to intervene.

Fortunately, the local police inspector was a friend of the club. He detained the young players only long enough to make a phone call to secretary Joe Eaton to explain the circumstances and give reassurances that the team's star forward was being driven home to his digs. Manager Raich Carter had been visiting his wife's family in Hull on Christmas Day and had stayed overnight in the city. Early on Boxing Day morning, Joe Eaton rang him to explain what had happened in the early hours. Given that Waggy was due to play the next day the events had been a serious breach of discipline.

Carter was not happy on hearing about Waggy's exploits with the local constabulary. He demanded the player be in his office by noon, just three hours before the game. After a fatherly chat, bordering on a dressing down, Waggy was told that he would not be playing in the side that day. Poleaxed by Carter's decision, he spluttered: 'You can't leave me out boss!' The crowd were astounded to find their star larker not on the pitch that day and entirely unimpressed when their side went down 1-0.

David Coates was in the Mansfield team that day and recalls what happened as the defeated Stags trudged off the pitch towards the tunnel: 'Peter Morris – who'd also been dropped that day – and the Wag were standing close by the tunnel as we came off. I heard Waggy shout that he thought I was man of the match and that it would be the last time Raich would leave him out!'

Waggy's prediction almost came true. The fact he was left out of the away game against Colchester on 23 March was further evidence of Carter's paternal concern for Waggy's welfare. He'd let it be known that he feared Colchester's tactics on the day would include making the player a target for some rough handling.

Joe Eaton recalls a knock on the office door a couple of days after the Rochdale game. In came Waggy to speak to a still-upset Carter. 'You are going to play me in the next match, aren't you boss?' gulped the player. 'Don't know yet boy,' came the reply. Carter almost invariably referred to Waggy as 'boy' and occasionally 'son'. In fact, having firmly made the points about discipline, Carter relented but half-jokingly announced that he might impose a fine. Waggy's response was to try and do a deal to offset the fine by scoring goals instead. Judging by his goalscoring record, it is very easy to see how Waggy could have bought himself a great deal of immunity from fines had the principle been accepted.

Ken recalls a sequel to the dance hall incident. One morning he'd arrived for training at Field Mill. Before the session started Carter collared his protégé: 'Raich said me: "You're not training this morning boy. You're coming with me." He then told me that I had come from a mining community where most people had to work hard in poor conditions, with little prospect of change. He told me that I had a chance to make something of myself. He didn't want me to spoil it through indiscipline. Then we went to a local hospital full of children with disabilities. They were over the moon to see us. Raich said to me: "Take a good look. One of the greatest gifts in life is to be born normal. You have a great gift – don't waste it!" I never forgot that lesson throughout my life. I looked up to Raich. He kept in touch with me throughout my career. There was no better player. As a man, he also had some great qualities.'

Joe Eaton acknowledges that thereafter, Ken made terrific progress at Mansfield. Carter had been adamant that if he found the right club, it was inevitable that Waggy would play for England. The maestro himself had identified something special in the young player. Such talents needed time to develop. It was also a matter of reaching the right understanding with others in the team.

The Carter–Wagstaff relationship was special. Joe, who worked closely with Carter, felt that the maestro saw something of himself in the emerging star. He almost took a fatherly interest in Waggy's career. Other players were in awe of their manager and his reputation. It wasn't a problem for Ken who would not hesitate to go in and speak to Raich.

One player with business in the office once knocked on the manager's door, full of trepidation, only to find Waggy sitting on a corner of the desk. The youngster greeted

Waggy made an instant impact for Mansfield, creating panic and havoc in the opposition's penalty area.

the more experienced player with: "Alright there son, how are you doing?" Carter managed to keep his composure – but later confided that he was highly amused by Waggy's cheek.

Ken's sense of humour spilled over from time to time in the form of various pranks. The classic bucket of water over the door caught one or two out with soakings. Even the groundsman fell for one of the Wag's tricks after he'd left his lawn mower unattended during a tea break. On his return, the machine was mysteriously lifeless. After countless attempts to re-start the machine, the groundsman was puffing and as red as a beetroot. At this point, Ken asked: 'Is everything okay?' In that instant, the groundsman twigged what had happened and realised exactly who had removed the spark lead from the plug!

At one point the Wag was put in digs with Dennis Wright, the club groundsman and part-time barman at a local working men's club. Fed up with Waggy's cheek, one day in a passageway at the rear of the club, Dennis playfully threatened to thump him unless

A delighted Ken meets up with David, a long-standing Stags supporter. David was present at Ken's first Field Mill game and has supported the side ever since. He shared the magic moment when Ken was presented with the award for the club's most popular player of all time.

it stopped. When it continued unabated, the ex-Mansfield 'keeper took a swipe. In a flash, Waggy ducked and caused the veteran to connect with the wall! The tale was a cause of some amusement to the players who frequented the watering hole, especially when they noticed Dennis with his arm in a sling.

No less a victim of Waggy's humour, was Peter Morris. One day while coming off after training Waggy goaded his pal into having a try at clipping the ball through the open side of two swing doors – both with glass panes. Morris succeeded in getting the ball through a door – but unfortunately it was the glass pane of the closed door that ended up shattered. Joe Eaton also recalls Waggy's cheek: 'He'd come up to the office regularly and ask for some complimentary tickets for his relatives. I'd give him some and then he'd try to get a few more saying his gran or whoever was coming. Eventually, I'd let him have a few more on the condition he'd score some goals. He rarely let me down! Its hard to remember back all those years – but I think players would have been earning maybe £100 or so a week – plus the £2 for a win and £1 for a draw! I think in those days the League had a regulation restricting the win bonus that could be paid.'

January 1962 saw attendances at Field Mill on the up again in response to a three-match winning spell – with games against Doncaster Rovers, Colchester United and Workington. In that period, the Stags scored nine goals with only one against. Two defeats and two draws in February were a prelude to an eight-game marathon in March. It seemed there were no half measures for the Stags.

Four decent wins were matched in magnitude with a similar number of defeats – including a 6-1 away slogging at Bradford City. The rest of the season was played out in similar vein – but was at least marked by four Wagstaff goals in seven games. In that season, he'd played 42 games and scored 12 goals. Things were progressing steadily, but the best was yet to come.

One interesting statistic from that season was the number of goals Mansfield scored from the penalty spot – nine in total during that season alone! Waggy was aware of the tendency for players to fall down in the box in the hope the referee would point to the spot. In fact, Raich had made him aware of such 'dangers': 'When I started at Mansfield, Raich took me on to the back field to explain the technical side of being fouled. Obviously, cheating is an unacceptable practice, but if the full-back is unfairly having a go, unless there's a definite chance on, it seems a bit stupid killing yourself to stay on your feet. In actual fact, in terms of gamesmanship, it's also fair play to put the defender in a position where he may be vulnerable to committing a foul on the spur of the moment. I used to lean into them and touch the ball on a bit. Often, they'd compete too hard, find themselves off balance and suffer the consequences of frustration in the form of penalties and free kicks.'

Davis Coates confirms the skilful techniques that Waggy employed to frustrate defenders so that they committed a foul: 'I once saw Waggy run rings round a defender so much that in the end the player just dived and grabbed the ball, giving away a penalty! He could also lean into a player running after the ball, push it on – then over-balance by easing off. He'd then fall before the other guy. He was bloody good at it!'

4

Upwards and Onwards 1962–64

It was with renewed hope that just over 6,000 fans turned up at Field Mill on the opening day of the 1962/63 season. They had seen some improvement last term, but mid-table mediocrity was not their idea of Utopia. They demanded better. Football was one of their few sources of entertainment, but there were other ways to spend hard-earned wages.

Carter responded by putting Wagstaff on in the out-and-out centre forward role next to big Roy Chapman. It was clear that Waggy could score goals given the opportunity. He was also capable of laying them on for others. Chapman was a ball winner and powerful striker. The combination had great potential.

For the second season in succession, the Stags won their first game, with Waggy scoring the only goal in a hard-fought encounter. Fans waited intently for the result of the away game at Exeter, half expecting the worst after last season's seesaw form. In fact, on the crest of a Wagstaff hat-trick, Mansfield emerged victors. A further away win

From left to right, back row: C. Toon, W. Nimmo, C. Treharne, J. Gill, E. Cupitt. Middle row: S. Chapman, C. Askey, J. Weir, F. Durco, R. Rogers, D. Boner, A. Tyrer, T. Richards, I. Hollett. Front row: M. Jones, W. Humble, D. Coates, B. Hall, K. Wagstaff, P. Morris, C. Govan, A. Scanlon.

at Brentford was enough to tempt more than 11,000 fans to Field Mill for the clash against Exeter City. Wagstaff's strike was enough to take that game and his tally now stood at six goals in four games. He'd struck in every match so far.

In the next six games, Town extended their unbeaten run to 10 matches, finding the net 19 times with only seven against. The season had started with six straight wins and then three draws on the trot. It was promotion form. In the next game against Gillingham on 22 September, the stalemate had been settled by a Wagstaff goal.

If this was to be a promotion year, the points difference between a win and a draw could be crucial at the end of the season. It worked both ways and when Stockport County came to Field Mill at the end of September the points went up in smoke after a disappointing 1-0 defeat.

Tranmere Rovers provided the antidote for that unwelcome sting of defeat and obligingly fell to a 6-1 drubbing in front of almost 10,000 Mansfield fans. The faithful were now starting to believe that the season would at last bring hoped-for success. On 22 October, in front of a massive 16,679 gate, the Stags hammered Chesterfield 3-0. The game was illuminated by two brilliant Wagstaff strikes. This was a feat he repeated in the next game against Barrow. Not to be outdone, Roy Chapman matched Waggy's tally in what became a 5-0 annihilation.

After his retirement, from the game Raich Carter confided that during this period of time he'd been receiving regular phone calls from Tottenham's manager Bill Nicholson about Ken Wagstaff. Although Carter had every interest in keeping his protégé as part of Mansfield's building success story, he knew that the boy's talent deserved a higher level. The maestro was convinced that Waggy was good enough to play on the International stage. For now he would learn his trade at Field Mill.

In the third successive home game, Darlington were the visitors. Despite the Stags' position in the table and their two recent convincing victories, the attendance dropped to 7,417 – less than half that at the Chesterfield game. Those absent missed a 6-0 thriller that featured yet another two-goal performance from Wagstaff, who took his season's League tally to 14 League goals – six of which had come in the last three games.

At that point in the season, things certainly looked promising. Despite an away defeat at Southport and a draw at Newport County it was clear that the Town had the ingredients for success in place. However, due to the extreme weather conditions that winter, there was no league football played in a period from the end of December until early March. Town lost their last two games before the enforced break.

After the 2-1 home defeat against Brentford on 22 December, almost 10,000 fans would have been forgiven for wondering if it was all about to go off the boil once again. As chill winds blew and snow fell in abundance, Carter at least had a warming inner confidence that Waggy had shown what he could do. Now he just needed him to do it more often.

That season, the FA Cup had brought plenty of opportunity for Mansfield to indulge in some target practice. In the first round, Hounslow held the Stags to a 3-3 draw, but they were decimated 9-2 in the replay at Field Mill. Waggy scored in each of the games, which also featured goalscoring feats by Hollett and Roy Chapman. The next round also provided high-scoring excitement. This time, Crystal Palace held out in a 2-2 draw but were comprehensively defeated 7-2 at Field Mill. Having scored both Mansfield's goals in the first leg, Waggy went on to score a hat-trick in the replay. Unfortunately, on 9 January Ipswich Town brought the Wembley road show to a disappointing end by edging the extra goal in a five-goal thriller.

Due to the continuation of extreme weather conditions that year, it was the last game played for two months. However, the enforced lay off gave people time to reflect on the change in fortunes at Field Mill. In the space of two years, the side had gone from narrowly avoiding having to apply for re-election, to 14th place in the previous term. Now the side had clicked and had become an exciting free-scoring outfit.

The young guns were hitting the target consistently. In the 23 League games to the end of December they had scored 54 times. The defence had shown a good degree of composure, having maintained 11 clean sheets and conceded only 26 goals in that same period. David Coates waxes lyrical about the forwards, but about Waggy in particular: 'He could turn defenders inside out. He was highly skilled. He could turn in with the ball, then he'd switch back out again, so no matter which way the defender turned he'd switch the other way. He is the best player at that particular skill I have ever seen in my life. He'd just mesmerise them and leave them for dead.

'I've seen him, on the centre circle, meet a long kick out of defence and strike the ball on the volley fully 40 yards as an inch-perfect pass to a player on the wing. He did it with confidence and it just made you gasp. He could dribble, he could finish and he made more goals than the fantastic amount he scored himself. Taken together, it's what made him such a special player.

On 9 March, as Arctic conditions abated, Oldham were the visitors at Field Mill. The 4-2 Stags victory featured another superb Wagstaff hat-trick. The game demonstrated yet another facet of his skill. Having taken the ball to the dead-ball line, David Coates had cut the ball back at speed across goal in the hope a Mansfield player would be on hand.

With perfect balance, Waggy latched on to the waist-high ball and unceremoniously volleyed it into the net. It was an almost uncanny knack of repeatedly being in the right place at the right time. But it was more than that, because more often than not, the chance was converted with an ice coolness and confidence of touch that is rare to say the least.

In the week before the Oldham game, Waggy had lost the man who had plucked him from obscurity and guided his path into the professional game. Raich Carter had moved to take up the reins at Middlesbrough. It was a disappointment, but it did not deflect a focus on a return to the park after what had seemed like an eternity. Tommy Cummings took over the job and the quest for success continued.

In the two away games that followed, and despite a brace from Waggy in the second match, the Stags' tally of points was zero having twice been beaten 3-2. The forwards were certainly scoring the goals. Unfortunately they were now being conceded at a faster rate.

In March, a seven-game spell ended with three straight wins. In order to beat the fixture backlog, the next month saw 10 League matches played – half of them at home. The game on 6 April was memorable in that Southport were knocked for six after a four-goal blitz from Waggy.

Waggy scores for Mansfield Town against Coventry City.

He also found the net twice in each of the home games against Doncaster Rovers and Bradford City. Without doubt, he was the darling of the terraces. His partnership with Roy Chapman was a clear success, with the big forward himself making a significant mark on the scoresheet.

As the fans cheered the team's goals to the echo, they also had one eye on the League table. April had returned five wins, four defeats and a draw. Although May was nothing to write home about with defeats at Crewe and York spoiling the party, a 4-3 away victory at Hartlepool was followed by a 4-0 home win against Chester. The Stags were promoted, having finished in fourth place.

Waggy's goal tally that year in 44 League appearances that year was a remarkable 34 goals. His strike partner, Roy Chapman, managed just four less in the same number of appearances. As the season had worn on, top clubs were beating a path to Field Mill to watch the Wagstaff goalscoring machine in action. Rumours abounded that some clubs had been put off by reports of the player's drinking habits.

Certainly, he liked a beer but reports of excessive drinking were exaggerated. Many felt that the habit would get in the way of an otherwise glittering career. Others felt that it was a simple and harmless part of his casual and slightly undisciplined make up. It has been argued that, without those minor so-called 'flaws', he might not have displayed the same genius as a footballer. Despite being a known disciplinarian, Carter turned a blind eye to all but the more serious aspects of Waggy's lifestyle. Another point of speculation surrounded transfer fees. Now becoming hot property, Mansfield would only be tempted to part with one of their main assets if the price was right.

The 1963/64 season opened in grand style for the Stags with a 2-1 home win against Crewe Alexandra. A crowd of 8,813 saw Waggy score both goals. After two away defeats at the hands of Port Vale (0-1) and Crystal Palace (1-3) respectively, the team returned to winning ways with a 2-1 victory over Walsall thanks to goals by Ken Wagstaff and Roy Chapman.

After a draw against Port Vale, the side lost to Reading by the odd goal in a seven-goal thriller. It all came good in the next game as 16,560 fans saw Notts County on the receiving end of a 4-0 battering. After the next four games, involving two draws, a narrow defeat and a 3-0 victory, the side emerged with their home record still intact.

On 7 October, in the crowd of just over 10,000 for the home game against Shrewsbury were scouts from Manchester City, Stoke, West Bromwich Albion, both Sheffield clubs, Aston Villa and Southampton. Also at the game was Jackie Milburn of Ipswich. All eyes were on Wagstaff. He responded with two brilliantly taken second-half goals. The press were of one voice in proclaiming Waggy as the deciding factor. Less euphoric were the Field Mill fans. The last thing they wanted was to see their star forward transferred to another club.

In the next game, Waggy scored the deciding goal in the 1-0 victory over Queens Park Rangers. With a little more luck, he could have easily scored a hat-trick past the impressive young goalkeeper Peter Springett – son of former England goalkeeper Ron.

It wasn't just about the number of goals he was scoring. Waggy's style of play had endeared him to the masses. It was all made to look so easy. With lightning speed he could convert half chances into goals. Equally, his remarkable vision kept a steady flow of balls through to Roy Chapman – himself building an awesome reputation.

At the time, the Stags were in the process of building a new stand. Although their finances were far from solid, cash flow had been improving. Yet all football clubs have to have a clear focus on the business side of their operations. In talking to the press about speculation over a possible Wagstaff move, manager Tommy Cummings was open and honest in his comments. The club was not rich and the player represented the potential for significant profit. On the other hand, he was a significant asset to the playing strength and success on the field. His remarks reflected one of the eternal dilemmas in football. He said: 'This boy is not on offer, but it is known that we would have to listen if the right fee was mentioned. As a manager, of course, I don't want to part with him. But, apart from the cash, which we can use, I can quite truthfully say that it would not be fair to stand in the way of such a player.'

Still unbeaten at home, on 21 October Town faced Brentford – another club with their sights firmly trained on acquiring Waggy's services. Their greatest hopes and wildest fears were satisfied in one, as the effervescent striker handed out a lesson in his opportunism by snatching two superbly taken goals.

His first-half equaliser following a return pass from Hollett was pure magic. After once more falling into arrears, Waggy rescued the situation three minutes later with another well-taken goal. Five days later, he scored once more in another home draw against Colchester United.

The last game in October saw the Stags go down 4-0 away to Brentford. Despite having terrific fire-power up front, many argued that the side needed strengthening at wing-half. All in all, they were performing better than expected at the higher level. However, at times it was a struggle against some of the division's better sides.

Another away defeat was inflicted on 2 November when the Stags went down 3-0 at Watford. However, three days later at Field Mill, they made amends with a 4-1 hammering of Southend United. Roy Chapman scored a great hat-trick. It was on this day that Waggy became engaged to Celia Waterfall, a 19-year-old Doncaster secretary. In celebration, Ken scored a customary goal. It is still unclear what Roy Chapman was celebrating!

Waggy got his first sight of Boothferry Park in a Boxing Day 1963 clash against Hull City in front of 14,132 fans. Town lost 3-1 in a lively encounter. Two days later, in a return game at Field Mill, Waggy scored one of the goals in the Stags' 2-0 revenge. The boy's performance in both the games was impressive. Hull manager Cliff Britton was already aware of his growing potential, but the funds to bring such a player to Hull would require a tangible act of faith from the chairman. For now, the club was content to monitor progress.

January 1964 was a Spartan month for Stags' supporters with only a single home League match – a 2-1 victory against Reading. Away games at Peterborough and Walsall brought mixed fortunes in the form of one win and a defeat. A 3-1 defeat at the hands of Nottingham Forest in the Notts FA County Cup drew in 13,419 fans. Again, the match provided a stage for Waggy to demonstrate his considerable abilities. Forest were suitable impressed and their interest grew in the rising star.

On 8 February 1964, Town completed the double over Coventry City in front of 16,755 supporters – the biggest gate since the cup tie against Ipswich 13 months earlier. Although he didn't get on the scoresheet, Waggy had a decisive hand in the goals that sank the Division Three leaders.

The local press waxed lyrical about his talents and quoted one supporter voicing what was felt to be the general view of the crowd – 'If they sell him they'll sell half the team.' The win marked the end of an eight-game goal drought for the Stags' Roy Chapman, who collected a confidence-boosting brace after injury problems. The defeat was a bitter blow for Coventry manager Jimmy Hill.

Prior to the Coventry City game, rumours were rife that Brentford had made an approach. It was no secret that Middlesbrough and Everton had both been closely following the player's progress. Stags' manager Tommy Cummings was quoted in the local press: 'Brentford did ring up and ask if we would be prepared to let Wagstaff go in exchange for two players and a sum of money. The amount was not specified. But I am not interested in the two players they suggested. In any case we should never be keen to part with a player of Wagstaff's calibre. We don't want to lose him.'

Dream team: shortly before Cliff Britton signed Ken Wagstaff, David Coates advised the Hull City manager that Waggy (centre) and Chris Chilton (right) would form a great partnership.

A week later in another home game against promotion seeking Bournemouth, Waggy put the Stags ahead with a 56th-minute goal. The first half had been a ding-dong affair with both sides having good attempts on goal, not least Roy Chapman, Morris and Wagstaff who all went close.

Mansfield started the second half at a fast pace. Reward for their efforts came in the 56th minute. Finding space on the left, Waggy set off on a run towards the middle that ended with a drive that glanced off the 'keeper and rocketed into the net. Unfortunately, the Stags conceded a goal two minutes later with the defenders waiting for an offside whistle to blow. In singing the praises of Wagstaff's performance, the press enthusiastically reported another of his 'customary' goals.

Between 7 October and 9 March he scored 15 goals in 25 League games. It was, to say the least, a useful tally – given that the side were now operating in a higher division against stronger opposition.

On 20 April the Stags met Southend United away from home. Although they lost the game 2-1, the match shone light on yet another facet of Waggy's talent – an ability to read the game. The Southend goalkeeper had played the ball out short to the centre half just outside the area. Lurking a short distance away Waggy saw the body language of the player and understood in an instant that the ball will be turned back to the 'keeper. In a flash, almost a second before the pass was made, he raced to intercept, beat the 'keeper to the ball, rounded him and scored.

In the final nine games of the season, Waggy netted nine times, the side coasting to five victories with only two defeats. On three occasions the forwards chalked up four goals, with Waggy scoring a brace in three of the games. Overall, Town scored 20 goals, conceding only nine themselves. In that year, as a result of the strong finish to the season, they finished in a creditable seventh place. In 46 League appearances that season, Ken scored 29 goals for Mansfield. It had been another brilliant season for him.

1964/65 was to be Waggy's last season at Field Mill. The team started with a 4-1 defeat away to Bristol Rovers, but in typical style bounced back with two successive 4-1 home victories against Brentford and Oldham Athletic. Scouts were ever-present at games and Waggy continued to give them food for thought with goals in each of the wins.

The next five games were close encounters, with the Stags registering two wins, two defeats and a draw. More goals were scored in the following game at Peterborough United than had been scored by either side in all of the earlier games added together. The nine goal thriller ended in victory for the Stags with Wagstaff on the scoresheet along with Chapman (2), MacReady and Scanlon.

Already hot on the trail, Manchester City had a close encounter with Ken's goalscoring prowess in the Football League Cup when the Stags travelled to Maine Road on 22 September 1964. The closely fought second-round tie finished 5-3 to the visitors with goals from Chapman (2), Wagstaff, MacReady and Tyrer. With the exception of Tyrer, the same players had been on the scoresheet in the game against the Posh. In the next round, the Stags crashed out 3-2 away to Coventry City.

In four games, including the clash with Grimsby Town on 26 September, the Stags turned specialists in 2-2 draws, the exception being a home game against Scunthorpe where the odd goal tipped the balance in the Stags' favour.

October was to be Waggy's last full month at Field Mill. In 9 League games, he scored 4 times – his final goal for the club securing a draw against Shrewsbury Town on 3 November.

On 24 October, Waggy had turned out a useful performance at Boothferry Park, where Cliff Britton was on the look out for a partner for Chris Chilton. Although several clubs were still interested in the player, some were unable to find the funds. Former Stags manager Raich Carter had initially found himself in financial difficulty in respect of raising sufficient cash to bring his protégé to the North East. In the end some funds did materialise, but other moves were afoot.

Cliff Britton had been impressed with Wagstaff's skills. Without question, the player was able to score goals, especially when paired with a strong ball winner and front runner. He would be a perfect foil for Chris Chilton. In piecing together a successful front line, Britton was also on the look out for a skilful and fast winger and an intelligent player in the centre – able to score, but importantly to keep the strike duo supplied with the necessary ammunition. As time would tell, three pieces of the puzzle would be former Rotherham players, with roots similar to Ken Wagstaff.

A former Hull City player, David Coates had been a great friend of Jimmy Lodge, the Tigers' masseur. Both men had originated in the North East and had become friends. Although David was by then a player at Notts County, he was still in a perfect position to provide information on Wagstaff's background and potential.

The call came in the form of a telegram asking David to contact a Hull number between 7.30pm and 8pm, and to reverse the charges. The man answering the phone was none other than Hull City manager Cliff Britton. During the conversation, Britton asked for David's opinions on the player: 'I told Cliff that he was an exceptionally fine player, that he would score a lot of goals but that he would make even more. He can beat people and knows where all his colleagues are. In particular, he asked me if I felt he'd be a good partner for Chris Chilton. I knew Chris and felt it was a combination sent from heaven.'

The conversation then moved on to personal questions about Waggy's drinking habits. Britton was reputed to be strict on such matters: 'I told him that he wouldn't be able to stop Waggy having a drink – something he'd been doing since he'd been 14. It's in his lifestyle. I said that he was a happy-go-lucky character who loved playing football. He was pleased to hear that Ken had a girlfriend with marriage plans, possibly because of the calming influence that might offer.'

At that point the conversation ended. However, David had already strongly recommended his old friend to Newcastle United. When nothing appeared to be happening, he chased up his contact who confirmed that they had watched Wagstaff but had decided not to pursue the matter because he couldn't seem to head a ball: 'It was unbelievable. I told them the man was a genius. Later they tried to sign both Wagstaff and Chilton – but it was too late.'

Hull City's enquiries about Wagstaff even reached Middlesbrough manager Raich Carter – himself desperate to sign his protégé. Unfortunately, despite some success in the transfer market, it seemed he still did not have the funds at his disposal to make a move. Carter's wife Pat recalls what had happened: 'Raich and I were at a dinner dance in the North East when he was called to the telephone. It was Stan Kershaw, a Hull City director. Raich told him that Wagstaff would be worth every penny of the £40,000 being asked by Mansfield. Raich wanted to sign him – but it wasn't possible at that time.'

Britton moved in with a decisive offer of £40,000 for Wagstaff, ahead of the glamour clubs who were procrastinating on rumour and hovering on lesser sums. Ken recalls receiving word that there was interest in him from Hull City. He was told simply: 'Get your suit on.' Together with manager Tommy Cummings and secretary Joe Eaton, Waggy travelled to Hull for talks with Cliff Britton and chairman Harold Needler. Once the deal was settled, the men enjoyed a meal together and finally walked to the car park chatting.

Waggy's eyes fastened on a beautiful sports car owned by the millionaire chairman. Seeing the boy's interest, Needler said: 'Score me 30 goals this season and I'll buy you one of those.' Quick as a flash, the pensive striker replied: 'That's not impossible Mr Needler.' The remark brought an inner smile from the Mansfield secretary, who realised only too well just how far the Hull chairman had stuck his neck out on that one!

Ken Wagstaff pictured at Boothferry Park, Hull, after signing for City on 12 November 1964.

Looking back at Waggy's time at Mansfield, Joe Eaton still enthuses about the player's personality and skills: 'Ken was a terrific finisher. For a lad of his age, he had amazing strength. You couldn't just knock him off the ball. He was a cheeky player.'

One retired Mansfield spectator had a particularly interesting anecdote to tell about the player who is still revered in the town: 'I once saw Ken Wagstaff do a one-two with the post to beat one 'keeper. He'd shot in the narrowest of angles past a diving goalie. The ball rebounded and there was Waggy to take the return and score with the 'keeper looking on bemused!'

Throughout his time at Mansfield, during which he scored 108 goals in 199 matches, Ken Wagstaff never played a single game in the reserves. When he moved to Hull, the Field Mill fans were gutted. They never forgot those goals, his character or the exceptional skills he displayed.

For Ken, it was time to leave behind the wonderful memories at Field Mill and take up a new challenge in Hull, where there was a burning ambition for success. As he travelled north, a master plan was coming together at Boothferry Park. It would lead to great times ahead. For now, Ken set about finding accommodation and settling down.

5

Britton's New Boys 1964/65

Waggy made his debut for Hull City at home against Exeter on Saturday 21 November 1964 – three days before his 22nd birthday. It was his 200th League appearance. The Tigers were mid-table in Division Three, having recently suffered two consecutive defeats to Grimsby Town (0-3) and Peterborough United (0-2). So far that season, they had scored 34 goals in the League with 27 against. That record had been flattered by a 7-0 home win over Barnsley in early October featuring four goals from Chris Chilton – and three from inside forward Ray Henderson.

Chilton's goal tally of 12 so far that season had also included a hat-trick in the 3-1 away win against Brentford. He was clearly a centre forward with great talent. The manager's job was to bring together a blend of players that could gain promotion and form the basis of an assault on winning the ultimate aim of Division One football for the club. For a city the size of Hull it was an achievement that was long overdue.

Hull's manager was a sound disciplinarian. A former Everton half-back, Cliff Britton had played for England alongside Joe Mercer and Stan Cullis – men who themselves went on to carve out brilliant careers in management. But it was Britton that first flew the flag, taking Burnley to promotion as well as a Cup Final appearance in 1946/47. A subsequent spell at Everton saw them hang on to top-flight status for two years before being relegated.

With the manager locked into a youth policy that spurned big spending in the transfer market, it was three long years before the Merseysiders again tasted Division One football. His poor relationship with the board was centred on his unwillingness to spend money. Eventually, he left in a sea of acrimony. Shortly afterwards, he joined Preston – again placing great emphasis on developing a sound youth policy. In a five-year spell, the team had challenged for the League championship. However, they were relegated in the 1960/61 season and Britton resigned.

Nonetheless, his management style and general philosophy appealed to Hull's ambitious chairman Harold Needler who

Hull City match programme for Ken Wagstaff's debut game.

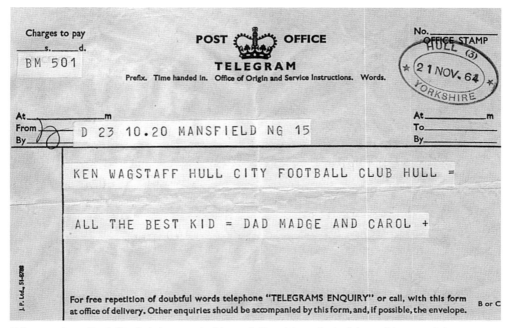

Telegram from Dad: Ken's father marks his son's Boothferry Park debut with a special message.

was looking for sustainable success and future development. The promised combination of a solid defence and the introduction of youth had been successful elsewhere.

Under Cliff Britton, sound discipline and adherence to principles became the norm. Players were not allowed to drink before a game and the dressing room was essentially out of bounds to the board. His approach was methodical and meticulous. The players came to respect this style – particularly in the context of the success it was to bring.

The men to execute the theory were brought together in a carefully thought-through plan. A central part of the strategy was the Chilton and Wagstaff strike force. Each had special talents and the combination was born in heaven. In general, Chilton had a more direct style using strength and height to power past defenders or to head a ball with great skill. He had come through the ranks at the club having arrived as a complete rookie from local non-League football.

Wagstaff was a master at reading the game. He used guile to move into space, beat defenders and outwit 'keepers. His finishing was probably without parallel, but at least on a par with that of Jimmy Greaves. Waggy's reputation of scoring goals was matched only by his record of laying them on for others.

Maurice Swan shared the green jersey with Mike Williams. He'd come to the club in June 1963 from Cardiff City. In time, he would earn the confidence of his team-mates. Waggy described him as 'a competent 'keeper and a safe pair of hands.' In the same month, Britton signed Dennis Butler from Chelsea. His partnership with full-back Andy Davidson proved to be long and successful. Davidson had made his debut in

Hull City manager Cliff Britton pictured near to the tunnel at Boothferry Park. He is standing in front of the nameplate taken from the stream engine that once bore the club's name.

September 1952. He had a reputation for his uncompromising tackles and as a solid leader on the field.

Although he'd joined the club in 1953, Les Collinson was still a force to be reckoned with in midfield. His powerful shooting, solid defensive play and attacking forward runs frequently brought fire to matches. It was no surprise when Wrexham-born Alan Jarvis arrived at Boothferry Park in May 1964. While he was the manager at Preston North End, Cliff Britton had already made moves to sign the player. Unfortunately, Everton held out greater promise and the bid failed. However, Britton persevered and finally brought him to Hull.

Mick Milner was a local lad come good, signing for City two years later. He missed only five League games in the 1964/65 term and was an ever-present the following year. Gerry Summers pre-dated Waggy at the club by only seven months, his arrival from Sheffield United being part of Britton's building project. His experience in midfield helped mould the emerging shape of the team.

Billy Wilkinson became a professional footballer with Hull City in May 1962, having previously spent some time as an amateur with Middlesbrough. He was at home almost anywhere on the park, but usually in midfield or at inside forward.

Terry Health came on to the Boothferry scene in May 1964 from Leicester City. He made only a few appearances for the Tigers but he was to play a decisive part in a memorable game against Nottingham Forest in the Tigers' 1965/66 giant-killing FA Cup run. Chris Simpkin, who'd made his debut in 1962, had been with the club as a junior. Initially perceived as a forward, he eventually came into his own as hard-tackling, attacking half-back.

Doug Clarke, the flying winger, had been with City since November 1955. His powerful runs down the wing over the years had brought goals aplenty – but his moon was on the wane and soon after Waggy joined the club, he gave way to a small bright star wandering in the firmament. John McSeveney was a wily Scot with a steely determination. In the 1962/63 season 'Jock' had actually outscored the great 'Chillo' with 22 goals from 39 games. He could operate on either wing and could kick with either foot.

In terms of style, the team essentially played a 4-4-2 style – often with the left-winger coming short. They were repeatedly drilled in positional play, intelligent use of space and the need to transfer the ball to the strike duo.

On his debut against Exeter in front of 11,765 fans, Waggy scored his first goal for the club in a pleasing 3-1 victory. He was again on the scoresheet just a week later, albeit in an away defeat at Oldham Athletic. On a sour note, the possibility of FA Cup glory soon disappeared following a home draw against Lincoln City during the course of which Waggy took a knock on the ankle. The Tigers lost 3-1 in the replay at Sincil Bank.

However, Waggy continued to score in every League game since joining the club by netting in a 1-1 home draw against Watford on 12 December. If the fans were already impressed with the new boy, they had seen nothing yet. In a 3-1 away win at Workington, Chilton netted twice with McSeveney also on the scoresheet.

Four days later, Ken was married to Celia. They'd originally met when she had come to interview him at Doncaster Rovers' ground. Instead of a honeymoon in some far-off paradise, the exotic Boxing Day location turned out to be Port Vale where the Tigers roasted the opposition 3-0 – with the spoils shared by Wagstaff, Chilton and Clarke.

Back at Boothferry Park 12,468 fans, more than double the previous gate, turned out to witness the demolition of Port Vale. Wagstaff took the game by the scruff of the neck with a brilliant hat-trick. A week later Colchester United fared little better. In their 5-1 drubbing, Waggy netted twice with Chilton, Henderson and McSeveney completing the rout.

Hull City *v.* Watford, 12 December 1964. Ken Wagstaff battles for the ball in an aerial duel inside the box during a 1-1 draw at Boothferry Park.

Winning was by now becoming a habit and the 9 January 3-2 victory at AFC Bournemouth took City's tally to five wins in a row. Chilton had found the net twice in that game and Waggy had scored his customary goal. In eight League matches, with only a single draw recorded, the Tigers had lost only one game. It was promotion form. The broad smiles in the Directors' Box said it all. Almost 17,000 fans had attended the Colchester game and there was a buzz about the ground again as the club improved its position in the Division Three table.

Twenty-four thousand fans turned up at Boothferry Park on 16 January 1965. The halcyon days appeared to be coming round once more. Confidence was running high.

Hull City players preparing for the top-of-the-table clash with Bristol Rovers on 30 January 1965. Chris Chilton, Les Collinson, Mike Williams, Ken Wagstaff and John McSeveney. City won 3-2 with goals from Chilton, McSeveney, Wagstaff.

Although Gillingham refused to lie down, at least the Tigers took a point, with yet another goal from Waggy – his already awesome reputation growing by the game.

The month saw two additions to Britton's squad – both players costing £40,000. Ken Houghton's arrival from Rotherham provided Ken Wagstaff with a connection to his abortive playing days at the club. Houghton was regarded as a creative and powerful player who regularly found the net. His vision and stylish play brought cohesion to the front line and an important alliance with Ian Butler – another signing from Rotherham! Butler's speed and trickery on the left wing led to the provision of accurate crosses for Chilton and Wagstaff to convert. Scoring goals was also a Butler forte. McSeveney switched wings and long-serving Doug Clarke gave way in favour of a revised line-up. Word of City's success was spreading like wildfire. More than 28,000 turned out for the Bristol Rovers game on 30 January, following another away win at Bristol City a week earlier when Waggy had added yet another brace to his record. Fans reading the local *Sports Mail Green* were now starting to simply look for how many he'd scored – almost taking yet another victory for granted!

In scoring two goals, Rovers made some attempt at forcing a draw, but Chilton, McSeveney and Wagstaff had other ideas. It brought Waggy's total to 14 goals in 11 League games. The team was still unbeaten at home since he'd joined the club, with only a single away defeat to spoil the record. February brought three wins and a goalless draw. The 4-0 away win at Shrewsbury demonstrated the side's great fire-power and featured Ian Butler's first goal for the club. Having only scored once, it was a relatively dry month for Waggy, but his part in team play helped Chilton continue his scoring success story. Chillo's League tally since Waggy's arrival had been 11 goals. The pair were working well together and converting the partnership into a successful goalscoring machine.

In March, Waggy averaged a goal a game. Having missed the 6 March match against Bristol Rovers he scored twice in the home derby against Grimsby Town. Games with the Mariners were always hard-fought and a draw satisfied fans on both banks of the Humber. The bumper attendance reflected the Tigers' continuing popularity and gave Hull City Chairman Harold Needler great heart that his investments were paying off handsomely.

Although the Tigers ended their 15-match unbeaten spell with the defeat at Peterborough – despite a Wagstaff strike – the month ended with the team doing the double over Bournemouth with a brace from Ken Houghton. The March tally was one win and two draws from four games. With spring in the air, the Tigers started April in fine style with an away win at Exeter to complete the double over the Grecians. Waggy found the mark, both in that game and in the 3-3 draw at Walsall. As the season drew to a close, the Tigers beat Oldham at Boothferry Park and then fell to a narrow away defeat at Southend.

On 17 April the Tigers went to Mansfield. Playing again at Field Mill was an emotional occasion for Ken. It had been a six-month absence that had seen his awesome reputation grow still more in the amber and black. He had little to prove to the 19,500 fans who turned out to see their former centre-forward. It was a remarkable home attendance, swelled in some small measure by travelling Hull fans.

Waggy did manage to get his name on the scoresheet. In all his time at Field Mill, he had never scored with his head. Although the Tigers were beaten 2-1, it was with some irony that the Stags noticed just how Waggy's goal had been scored. It prompted their manager to say: 'Fancy that, all those games with us and he hardly used his head. Then he comes back and scores with a header!'

At this point in the season, the Tigers were still in with a shout for promotion. Victory against the Stags could well have made all the difference. In the next game the Tigers were held to a 0-0 draw by Southend United at Boothferry Park. Again with some irony, the 'keeper that denied the Tigers in that game was Ian McKechnie – destined to join them in the not-too-distant future.

Ken Wagstaff sends 'keeper Davies the wrong way from the penalty spot to score the first of three goals against Port Vale. The hat-trick made him the leading scorer in Division Three with 20 goals – 13 with Mansfield prior to his transfer. A goal by Henderson completed the Tigers' scoring in a 4-0 blitz.

The Easter programme left City placed third in the promotion ladder with one game left. Above the Tigers were Carlisle United and Mansfield – both teams still having to meet. Following the leader pack came Gillingham, Brentford and Bristol City – all with games in hand. Hull finished the season in great style with a win against Brentford. Waggy took his tally to 23 goals in 25 League appearances.

However, when the final whistle blew on the season, Carlisle were promoted Champions on 60 points, with Bristol as runners up on 59 points – pipping Mansfield on the same number. The Tigers slumped to fourth place on 58 points. A win at Mansfield would have brought City sufficient points to have taken them into Division Two. That those points were lost through Waggy's sense of humour is arguable – but an issue that wasn't entirely lost on the player himself: 'The papers said that the 'keeper had a lot of luck in saving shots from Chillo and me. Maybe that's true – but there's

Waggy heads home. Ken Wagstaff powers a rare header goalwards.

more to it than that. Before the game, I'd told Treharne that I was going to put two through his legs. When the chances to score came, I could have slotted them in either side but on both occasions tried to nutmeg him. He was lucky to save them but I should have concentrated on the result and not on winding up my old mate!'

Former Mansfield player David Coates was aware of what happened and has a clear view about it: 'I spoke to some of the Hull players afterwards at social events. Some of them blamed Ken for missing promotion that year. Frankly, I had to remind them of where they were before he arrived at Hull and just how many goals he had scored for them. Ken has a terrific sense of humour and great cheek. Maybe he should have buried the chances in the net instead of messing around but he certainly made up for it the following year!'

The season ended with a friendly game against an All Star XI. In a 17-goal bonanza, the Tigers shaded it by a single goal. The game featured a Wagstaff hat-trick, with two goals apiece for Chilton and Houghton. John McSeveney and Ian Butler completed the list of goalscorers. It had been a remarkable first season for Waggy. In the 26 League games played since his arrival, the Tigers had recorded 15 wins and 7 draws, with only 4 defeats – all by a 2-1 margin and all away from home.

With 57 League goals to their credit in that period, the side had conceded only 30. It was a remarkable testimony to Britton's new boys in a first season when lesser form would have been forgiven. It can take a considerable time for players to find understandings. The reality was that the Chilton and Wagstaff partnership had worked instantly: 'Chillo and I more or less gelled straight away. The secret was in the effective use of space. Cliff pointed out that it was no use just being up in the box. Defenders would simply pick us up. He always said that the aim was to get the ball to Chris and me. After that, his job was finished. He said I'm not going to tell you how to play. That's why we bought you.'

The partnership between Chilton and Wagstaff was one based on mutual respect, both in personal terms and on the field of play. Top players do not always have such a liking for each other. That they hit it off so well was important to the continuing understanding that was translated arguably into the most effective strike partnership in the entire Football League.

As new players were introduced, service to the forwards improved. Time would hone the team's performance still further. The best was yet to come.

6

Glory Days 1965/66

The Tigers reported for pre-season training in July 1965, full of optimism and confidence. The manager had put together a great combination of young talent in the front line. In midfield, there was a blend of solidity and creativity. At the back was a wealth of experience, not least in goal. The key to success was to ensure high levels of fitness, maintain defensive discipline and develop fluidity and understandings throughout the side. Waggy recalls the training schedules at the club: 'During the season we'd start off on Mondays with a warm-up game of five-a-side. In the afternoon between 2pm and 3.30pm we'd maybe practise free kicks in the gym. On Tuesdays, we'd do some track work round the Boothferry park pitch and then in the afternoon we'd work in the gym.

Hull City, 1965/66 season. From left to right, back row: Alan Jarvis, Andy Davidson, Mike Milner, Maurice Swan, Chris Simpkin, Mick Brown, Terry Heath. Front row: Ray Henderson, Ken Wagstaff, Chris Chilton, Ken Houghton, Ian Butler.

Hull City *v.* Swansea, 1 January 1966. Waggy scores off the crossbar with Chilton (left) and Houghton (right) looking on.

The next day we'd do some running work and hard training for an hour. That afternoon, we'd play a game on the full-size pitch. It varied according to when games were being played but that's the flavour of it.

The 1965/66 League season started with a home derby clash against Scunthorpe United. The match attracted almost 19,000 fans. Games with the Iron were nearly always highly charged and closely fought affairs. Rivalry on the terraces was always emotional and victory was important in both camps. In adding two goals to Ken Houghton's brilliantly taken strike, Waggy helped seal a 3-2 victory and found himself ever closer to the hearts and minds of the success-starved Hull City fans.

August ended with the Tigers unbeaten, having drawn at Watford and won by a one-goal margin at Brighton and Hove Albion, with Wagstaff and Henderson finding the net. More than 23,000 fans then saw Waggy extend the side's unbeaten run with a goal against Swindon Town. However, that game aside, September proved to be a disappointing month for the Tigers with defeats against Queens Park Rangers and York City.

Waggy in training in the 1965/66 season.

Waggy failed to score in yet another visit to his old club Mansfield Town on 11 September. However, this time it was the Tigers that came away victorious.

An early exit from the Football League Cup after a 2-2 home draw against Derby County was of little consequence to the big picture. In the 4-3 defeat, Wagstaff, Chilton and Simpkin had all found the net. September ended with a high-scoring draw at Reading. From eight League games the Tigers had won four, drawn two and lost two. So far, so good – but they could do better.

In seven games during October they scored 19 times with 13 conceded. The forwards were scoring goals with alacrity, but the bucket was leaking just a little too fast. In all League games since the season had started, the side was conceding an average of almost two goals in every game. The forwards had struck 33 times in 15 matches – including three against Bournemouth – a side they had beaten three times in the League that year, if not the season! The month marked the transfer of Gerry Summers to Walsall.

Notable results in October included a 4-1 away victory at Exeter on the second day of the month. Four days later, Oldham received a 5-1 caning at Boothferry Park with more than 17,000 fans in an ecstatic mood. The match featured a Chilton hat-trick with goals from Waggy and Ken Houghton adding to the festivities.

Games against Swansea and Workington on the 9th and 22nd respectively were setbacks with seven goals conceded and only two scored in reply. Sandwiched between those games was a draw against Oldham, which was followed by a 3-2 victory at Walsall. Despite the introduction of the immensely talented Alan Jarvis to the team at the Workington game, in some quarters there were continued murmurings about the defence.

The team's defensive record in the League improved during November with the Tigers notching up wins against Southend and Watford. Waggy and Ian Butler scored in a 2-2 draw at Shrewsbury. The home derby match against Grimsby Town on 27 November attracted another bumper gate. In an extremely tight contest, Waggy prevented a Grimsby victory with yet another inspired strike. Having scored eight goals in the League, the Tigers had conceded only four. It was an improvement.

December began brightly with a 6-1 win at Bristol Rovers. A week later Walsall went down 4-2 on the receiving end of an Ian Butler hat-trick. 'Buck scored a brilliant hat-trick against Walsall,' Waggy recalls. 'Although he was getting the crosses in to Chillo and me, sometimes he'd cut in and take defenders on before cracking in a shot. It gave us something different to throw at the opposition to keep them guessing.'

The year finished with two games on successive days against Millwall. The sides shared the spoils with a win each – the Tigers conceding three in the away leg on 28 December. In fact, Millwall were a very good side that season and won promotion as runners-up.

As a team, the players were a close unit and there was a good atmosphere in the dressing room. Many would mix socially. Reports of uncontrolled drinking were well wide of the mark. Waggy's reputation was exaggerated by rumours that grew in the telling. The reality was that he enjoyed socializing, but in moderation, rather than excess. In dismissing reports of excessive drinking, Chris Simpkin revealed that the wild speculation was largely complete rubbish. However, one tale that has largely gone untold relates to his late-evening visit to a large Ferensway dance hall following a day of shooting in the country. It seems he hadn't had the time to go home and change and so arrived at the entrance dressed in all the shooting gear – complete with shotgun!

'I used to go shooting with Andy Davidson and Doug Clarke,' says Waggy. 'Andy was a bit of a character. He'd sometimes have a practice blast into the sky out of the car window as we drove there. One day, we'd had a long day on a friend's farm and on the way back I decided to go straight to the nightspot. Nobody said anything when I walked in carrying a shotgun. The manager kindly kept it in his office. It was in a case. He also lent me a suit. Unfortunately, it was one of those with silk braid down the leg, but it was better than wearing all the shooting gear.'

Hull City manager Cliff Britton uses the half-time break in a pre-season private practice game at Boothferry Park to talk tactics with the first team. As a result they improved on their first-half single-goal advantage and turned it into an 8-2 victory.

Waggy tests the Grimsby defence during the 1-1 draw on 27 November 1965.

On another occasion, the players went for a night out together, moving from place to place 'so that the landlords didn't accuse us of favouritism.' As the night wore on, Billy Wilkinson settled down in one of the clubs they'd visited. Seeing he was okay where he was, his team-mates said they would pop back later to collect him. Unfortunately, they completely forgot!

'We all went home and off to bed. When my phone rang at 5am I was at first shocked to hear Billy's girlfriend asking where he was. Then I realised that we'd left him in a club promising to go back after we'd done the rounds. I went back to the place where we'd left him – and he was still sitting there waiting for us!'

In the first three months of 1966, the Tigers had their sights set firmly on going up. After a shaky start to the season, question marks over the defence had all but evaporated. In 11 League games during early 1966 they conceded only 10 goals and managed six clean sheets. The side had scored 30 goals with 10 of those going to Waggy, six to Ken Houghton, four apiece to Chris Chilton, Ian Butler and Ray Henderson and one to Alan Jarvis with an unsung effort attributed as an own goal. The side was firing on all cylinders.

During that period, there were several games of particular note. On New Year's Day, almost 23,000 fans saw Swansea hammered 4-1, with a brace of goals coming from Wagstaff. On 15 January, Workington were blasted 6-0. On 29 January City did the double on Scunthorpe – the Iron managing only two in the six-goal bonanza. The Workington game was the first of a 14-game unbeaten League run for the Tigers.

On 26 February the visitors to Boothferry Park suffered a 4-0 mauling. Although still sentimentally attached to his old club, Waggy didn't let the feelings get in the way of his two-goal contribution to Mansfield's bad day out. Gillingham were the next scalp, falling 1-0 to a Wagstaff goal.

The 1965/66 FA Cup run had started on 13 November with a 3-2 first round victory at Bradford Park Avenue. Gateshead were dispatched in the next round with a 4-0 home win. During the three home ties that followed against Southampton, Nottingham Forest and Southport, the Tigers scored five goals without reply.

In the sixth round, City faced Chelsea away. That epic battle was described in the first chapter. The 2-2 draw remains one of the classic games in the club's history. Ken Wagstaff's two late goals were still the topic of conversation thirty years later. Had one clear penalty been awarded and but for the woodwork in the dying seconds of the game, City would have been in the next round. Instead, it was on to a replay at Boothferry Park. For the first tie, the Tigers were better prepared than their Division One opposition. It was to be a different story for the return contest.

The evening replay, against Chelsea at Boothferry Park on Thursday 31 March 1966, set the city buzzing with anticipation and excitement. Midfielder Chris Simpkin recalls walking into the ground a couple of hours before kick off: 'It was sensational. Two hours before kick off the ground was almost full. The roads outside were just normal – but inside the ground the atmosphere was electric. Only those with reserved seats came later. Others had been queuing since early morning. Eventually, as we walked on to the pitch, there was the most enormous roar. I had never experienced anything like it before or since at Boothferry Park.'

The earlier match at Stamford Bridge had raised expectations ever higher among fans. Many were even more certain that the Tigers could actually progress through the competition and possibly reach the final for the first time in their history. Despite being the two-goal hero the previous Saturday, Waggy was less sure about the outcome, even allowing for home advantage: 'Our best chance came in the first game when they underestimated what we could do. Tommy Docherty got the shock of his life. After that, he tightened up considerably on Chillo and me. They were far more physical. Peter Osgood gave them the advantage. He didn't play in the first game. He was good on the

Grimsby full-back Taylor heads the ball away with Wagstaff challenging – 27 November 1965.

Goalkeeper Geoff Sidebottom comes to the Irons' rescue in the match on 29 January 1966. The final score was Hull City 4 Scunthorpe United 2.

ball and tore us apart a little at the back. In hindsight we may have been better man-for-man marking him.

City lost the replay 3-1, but they were not disgraced. Chris Simpkin fired in a stunning consolation goal. The 30-yard drive, which must have been a prime contender for goal of the season, was unstoppable and ended up in the angle. With Chelsea out of their system and Cup dreams a fading memory, the Tigers were free to concentrate on chasing promotion. It seemed business as usual when Wagstaff and Houghton sank Oxford on 8 April.

The next day, Brentford fell victim to a four-goal Wagstaff *blitzkrieg* – the relegation-haunted home side at least grabbing two consolation goals. In reaching his hat-trick in the 55th minute Waggy equalled the record for away goals in a season. He went on to score a fourth in a performance that saw him use open spaces brilliantly. But for some superb goalkeeping, the Tigers could have doubled their tally.

Back at Boothferry Park on 11 April for the third League game in four days, the Tigers faced Oxford United once more in front of 31,992 spectators. Waggy recalls that: 'Oxford came for a point. They scored inside 30 seconds and that set them up to try and keep us out for the rest of the game. They were very negative but we needed the points badly so we had to go for it. Every time we got anywhere near, they just packed the area.'

Throughout the first half, the Tigers pounded away with Ian Butler on the wing trying to dance a path through the eight-man wall. In midfield, Houghton, Jarvis and Simpkin desperately tried to engineer openings but Oxford held out – buoyed by their early strike. The tension in the ground was palpable as the crowd willed the forwards to score. It was abundantly clear that it was going to take something special to counter United's spoiling tactics.

Six minutes from the interval, Henderson found himself on the ball and surrounded by the hacking feet of determined defenders. Sensing an opportunity opening up, Wagstaff found space just on the edge of the melee. In an instant, Henderson fed the ball through for Waggy to curve a left-foot shot away from the diving 'keeper and into the net, just inside the upright. It was his 30th goal of the season and on a par with Bill Bradbury's post-war record.

Oxford continued with their negative tactics throughout the second half and on occasions threatened to capitalise on defensive mistakes in the Tigers improved rearguard. Of late, they had maintained reasonably sound cover. However, desperate to take the game, they had shown vulnerability as Oxford tried to catch them on the break.

Two minutes from time and with the crowd in the West stand on the edge of their seats, Jarvis flighted an accurate free kick into the Oxford area. It was perfectly placed for Chilton to outwit Kyle and give the 'keeper no chance with a powerful and match-winning header into the net.

Yet again the duo of Chilton and Wagstaff had delivered the goods – a potent strike force at the head of an inventive, determined and skilful side well deserving of a place at the head of Division Three. With a game in hand over Millwall and two points clear, it was a reasonable happy side that took the next day off and waited for the result of games being played by their rivals on that day.

Hull City goalkeeper Maurice Swan turns photographer to capture the relaxed Hull City strike force just before the Chelsea cup game on 26 March 1966. From left to right: Ray Henderson, Ken Wagstaff, Chris Chilton, Ken Houghton, Dennis Butler.

69

In pensive mood: Hull City players in the gymnasium prior to the Chelsea FA Cup match at Stamford Bridge on 26 March 1966.

Division Three 1965/66 – The Run In

	P	W	D	L	F	A	Pts
HULL CITY	37	25	6	6	90	51	56
Millwall	38	22	10	6	64	36	54
QPR	34	19	8	7	76	47	46

Thereafter in seven League games from and including 11 April, Chris Chilton had scored eight goals – including a hat-trick in the 6-1 defeat of Exeter City. It emphasised the potency of the player who went on to become the Tigers' all-time record goalscorer. His partnership with Wagstaff was clearly delivering the goods. Seventeen goals had been scored in all during that period with ten in reply – a figure inflated by a 4-1 defeat away at Peterborough. The side were on the brink of success – just a little over a season after the blueprint was laid.

The away game against Bristol Rovers at Eastville on 6 May 1966 brought another vital win for Hull City, with goals by Wagstaff and Chilton securing the points. The victory clinched promotion, but not yet the championship. Waggy's goal was his 200th in the League and it finally took him past Bill Bradbury's 1958/59 record of 30 goals in a season. The strike came in the 11th minute as a pass through from Ken Houghton was headed delicately over the head of an advancing 'keeper.

It was also a night to remember for Chris Chilton who also scored and took his tally in the season to a personal best. Having made his debut in August 1960, Chillo had

Hull City versus Chelsea. Quarter-final replay at Boothferry Park, 31 March 1966. Peter Bonetti Ken Wagstaff and Peter Osgood tussle for possession.

Goalmouth action. FA Cup sixth round replay at Boothferry Park 31 March 1966. From left to right: Ron Harris, Ken Wagstaff, Peter Bonetti, Ray Henderson.

Goalmouth duel in the FA Cup quarter-final replay at Boothferry Park on Thursday 31 March 1966. Mike Milner is at full stretch as Chelsea's George Graham tries to push through.

already become the club's leading scorer in terms of cumulative goals. Ken recalls the milestone game: 'Chillo and I both had something to celebrate on that day. I can remember we went out that evening in Bristol down some cobbled street.'

Waggy's record spoke volumes for his strike rate. It represented a remarkable achievement, but one which he puts into perspective: 'Obviously, it was good to be breaking records, but the credit has to go to the others as well. We were a high-scoring side and the chances were coming up as part of the efforts from everybody.'

Hull City v. Oxford United, 11 April 1966. Wagstaff heads for goal in City's 2-1 win.

It was certainly the case that the side were performing well, but the player's skills were not being placed under a bushel by supporters. The cry 'Waggy, Waggy, Waggy' was being shouted by fans throughout the City in pubs and clubs and, in fact, any gathering where spirits were high. His goalscoring exploits and cheeky style had captured their imagination and their hearts. His name, and that of his strike partner Chris Chilton, became synonymous with achievement and success.

With a draw from the 10 May game at Bournemouth under their belts, the Tigers got revenge at home to Peterborough with a 2-1 win. Press reports after the game suggested that 'City according to local opinion play to a plan'. In the same column, the writer stated: 'I could see no plan in attack.' He went on to say: 'Nowhere outside Old Trafford and possibly Stoke is so much talent allowed so much free expression.'

In fact, the Tigers were one of the best-drilled sides in the country. In training session after training session, manager Cliff Britton had continued to inculcate an overall strategy aimed at getting the ball through to Chilton and Wagstaff. Chillo would act as a decoy opening up space for Wagstaff, or for Houghton and Simpkin moving in behind. If Chilton wasn't picked up he would deliver the bad news to goalkeepers himself. Of course, there was considerable invention in the Tigers' attack but a framework existed within which liberated talents flourished. When scenarios didn't go as expected there were fall-back strategies and always the freedom for any player to shoot when an opportunity arose. Waggy recalls: 'First and foremost Cliff was concerned with how we would play, rather than being bothered too much about the opposition. He'd get round to them later. Sometimes he'd adjust things to combat a particular threat and, if it was required, order man-to-man marking. One time we did it against John Toshack in a game at Cardiff and he scored a hat-trick inside 20 minutes!

'The mistake teams often make is to pass a ball to the forward already waiting in the space, with a defender already on him. Cliff insisted repeatedly that we hold back and only make a run when the ball was on its way. Obviously, we needed to have an idea of how the passing player was thinking and vice versa. We achieved it by learning various routines. We practised varying scenarios all the time in training.

'We knew that when the ball went to Simpkin and then to Frankie Banks and the two wingers went short that the ball was going to come over the top. So we never started to run until the ball was on its way into the space. That way you could get five or ten yards on the defender. Then he's got the problem. When their full-backs stayed back, we'd adapt and play it slightly differently – perhaps getting the ball out to the winger. If Butler went short and lost his marker, he'd get the ball. The midfielders would decide which way to play it. When Butler got the ball someone would go to the near post every time. Chris would go to the near or far post mostly. Usually Ken Houghton would hang back. We knew where everybody was. It takes time for a team to gel, but within a year or so it was second nature.

'Often there were fun times – especially with Ian Butler. He'd sometimes wind Chris up by dribbling away down the wing. Chris would make his run to the near post or whatever and then find Buck had changed his mind and was dribbling off somewhere else! It was a similar set up at Mansfield with Michael Stringfellow on the wing and big Roy Chapman in the middle knocking balls down to me.'

Championship-winning celebrations: the Lord Mayor shares a joke with Hull City players during the civic dinner to celebrate the Tigers' championship-winning campaign of 1965/66. From left to right: Mike Milner, Ken Wagstaff, Mike Williams, Terry Heath

Years later, Ian Butler explained why on odd occasions his normally incisive runs followed by pinpoint crosses were replaced by meandering journeys, with Chillo in the middle running around like an expectant hen: 'Nowadays players just whip crosses in whether there's anyone there or not. I tried to avoid sending in blind crosses. If there was nothing on I just kept the ball until I could pass it usefully. There was no point in just giving it to the opposition. Chillo was great because he was easy to pick out. He was an awesome player. When it got to Waggy, it was as good as in the net. I loved playing when we played forward. Later I ended up coming from deeper. It's a more difficult game pulling back and then having to cover greater distances with the same speed and energy over long periods.'

Within the general framework, the manager did not dictate to the forwards how they should score. His focus was on delivering the ball into the strike zone. Thereafter, he left the player to work on his own brand of magic.

Britton would regularly stop practice games and correct tactical mistakes. He was a stickler for making sure that balls to Waggy or Chillo were accurately placed on the correct side in relation to the defender. Day after day this was practised by the

A goal in 18 seconds: Hull City *v.* Gillingham, 9 March 1966. A devastatingly effective Wagstaff forces the ball past a Gillingham defender.

support players so that the strikers weren't placed at an immediate disadvantage in the battle up front. The weighting, placing, speed and direction of the passes were rehearsed again and again. In the end, the team was so finely tuned that it came as second nature. Set plays were worked out in advance so everyone knew what was expected.

In the same newspaper report on the Peterborough match, the writer asked: 'but can the defence move up a class? Last night for instance City might have been two goals down in the first 17 minutes.' It was a fair point, but it failed to acknowledge sufficiently that football is a team game and that some responsibilities for defence and attack rest in each and every player. In order to score goals, there is a need for forward play – often originating deep in defence.

Ken Houghton asserts that: 'Cliff Britton was a master tactician. We knew exactly what we had to do if we lost the ball to stop the opposition playing. Every player had his role determined.'

Augmenting Britton's extensive written reports on opposition teams were *ad hoc* contributions from Chris Simpkin. The player was a football enthusiast with an encyclopedic knowledge of players in all divisions. He would input his assessment of their strengths and weaknesses.

Despite the fact that the success of Hull City was a team effort, the media often focused on publicizing the goalscorers. Waggy acknowledges: 'It was true that the forwards tended to get the headlines. That's life I suppose. Often they'd recognise good play or solid defensive performances in the report somewhere, but it was the goalscorers that got the banner headlines. You could understand it if some of the players thought that was unfair. Without the midfield and defence – and I include the 'keepers in that – the forwards would never be in a position to score.'

Although Ken Wagstaff's reputation as a goalscorer was legend, the Peterborough game demonstrated his influence on making goals for other players, particularly the immensely talented Chris Chilton. It was a reciprocal arrangement because Chilton often placed balls in the path of his team-mate to convert. That Waggy's brilliant timing, rare skill, deceptive speed, amazing coolness and rare artistry ensured an incredible rate of success took nothing away from his partner's unselfish play. In fact, Chilton was a star in his own right and at times Waggy was his supporting act.

In the game against Peterborough, following a brilliant Houghton goal, Chilton had zipped in a stinging 20-yard drive to startle the 'keeper, who was forced to make a desperate one-handed save. As ever, Waggy was roving in and around the area seeking out vital space. When the ball came to him, in an act of typical awareness, he threaded the ball through to Chilton who was running unmarked on the edge of the Posh defence. The tall striker ran on to the perfectly placed pass and lashed a tremendous drive past the stunned Duff in goal. It was a goal worthy of the championship – yet more testimony to the potency of the Chillo and Waggy scoring machine.

The Tigers took the Division Three championship in the last game of the season at home to Southend United by virtue of an Ian Butler goal. It was a memorable and emotional occasion for the 30,371 fans packed into Boothferry Park. Ian Butler recalls: 'It was a difficult last game of the season, with the championship hanging on the result. We struggled to get through

CELEBRATION DINNER
in honour of
HULL CITY
FOOTBALL CLUB

Winners of the
SUNDAY MIRROR
GIANT-KILLER
CUP
1965-66

Royal Station Hotel, Hull, 17th May 1966

Programme for the Celebration Dinner in honour of Hull City – winners of the *Sunday Mirror* Giant-Killer Cup 1965/66.

their defence. Then I found myself on the edge of the box and decided to have a crack at goal. It flew into the bottom right side of the net. The feeling was fantastic. When the final whistle blew, the fans just crowded on the pitch round the Directors' Box. Cliff and the directors were delighted that their investments had paid off. We'd done it!'

Ken recalls his feelings on that day: 'It was a great feeling again. We'd gone up at Mansfield and now it was happening all over again at Hull City. We just couldn't wait for the next season to have a go at Division One. But for maybe a couple of signings, we thought we had the players to do it.'

In that promotion year, the city of Hull was elated. At last, the club was experiencing great success. They had gone up in grand style as champions. It was World Cup year and the competition was being staged in England. It was football, football all the way. To be a Hull City player in those halcyon days was to be a local hero. In honour of the season's achievements, on 22 July 1966 a dinner was held at the Grand Hotel in Scarborough. Players were presented with championship medals. Ian Butler recalls other perks of the team's success: 'We literally had the freedom of the city. We went to places and we'd be let in free of charge. It was a great feeling and we were raring to go in the new world of Division Two. We believed that we could go up yet again in the following year.'

One interesting sequel to the Hull promotion celebrations occurred in Torquay a short time afterwards. Former City winger Doug Clarke had found success with his new club. United had just that season been promoted from Division Four. On the team coach one day, Duggie suddenly became aware of a figure outside jumping up and down trying to attract his attention. Peering out through the steamed-up window, he realised that it was none other than his former team-mate Ken Wagstaff, on holiday in the resort. Within a few short minutes, Waggy had talked his way into the Torquay celebrations and became arguably the first player in the history of the Football League to enjoy two promotion dinners in the same season!

Final League Positions Division 3 1965/66

	P	W	D	L	F	A	W	D	L	F	A	Pts
1 HULL CITY	46	19	2	2	64	24	12	5	6	45	38	69
2 Millwall	46	19	4	0	47	13	8	7	8	29	30	65
3 QPR	46	16	3	4	62	29	8	6	9	33	36	57
4 Scunthorpe Utd	46	9	8	6	44	34	12	3	8	36	33	53
5 Workington	46	13	6	4	38	18	6	8	9	29	39	52
6 Gillingham	46	14	4	5	33	19	8	4	11	29	35	52
7 Swindon Town	46	11	8	4	43	18	8	5	10	31	30	51
8 Reading	46	13	5	5	36	19	6	8	9	34	44	51
9 Walsall	46	13	7	3	48	21	7	3	13	29	43	50
10 Shrewsbury T	46	13	7	3	48	22	6	4	13	25	42	49
11 Grimsby Town	46	15	6	2	47	25	2	7	14	21	37	47
12 Watford	46	12	4	7	33	19	5	9	9	22	32	47

The top 12 places. Source: *The Definitive Hull City.*

7

Going Close 1966/67

Now back in Division Two, the Tigers were in theory within a season of the Holy Grail of providing Division One football in the city of Hull. Despite the championship achievement, many felt that the side would benefit from a couple of signings in defence, particularly now that the team would be playing in a higher League. Although bringing in Ian McKechnie to help cover Maurice Swan in goal helped improve competition for the green jersey, some felt that the manager ought to have gone further with outfield acquisitions.

McKechnie was one of the great characters at the club. Originally he played on the left wing at Arsenal. Then, his remarkable goalkeeping skills became apparent during a practice game. He joined the Tigers in August 1966 and quickly established himself as the first-choice 'keeper. Waggy recalls some funny incidents during training involving

Hull City. From left to right, back row: Dennis Butler Alan Jarvis, Andy Davidson, Maurice Swan, Mike Milner, Chris Simpkin. Front row: Ray Henderson, Ken Wagstaff Chris Chilton, Ken Houghton, Ian Butler.

Tigers in training in 1966/67. From left to right, back row: Ken Wagstaff, John McSeveney, John Simpson (assistant trainer), Mike Milner, Chris Chilton, Andy Davidson.

Ian: 'The lads used to sing all the time. Ian had a remarkable likeness to Frankie Vaughan, so he'd often do us a solo on the coach. He was a real character. Once, we were having a practice game on the training ground, it was a cold day and there was snow on the pitch. We loved playing on snow. The lads were cracking in shots and because the ball was slippery, it was difficult for Ian to hold on to them. Cliff Britton was watching the play in his trilby and galoshes. He always rattled change in his trouser pocket. After a few balls had slipped through Ian's hands, he shouted across: "Ian, catch

Cup-tie training prior to the third-round tie against Portsmouth on 28 January 1967. From left to right: (Horses) Ian McKechnie, Ian Butler, Ken Wagstaff, Chris Chilton, Alan Jarvis, Andy Davidson. (Jockeys) Billy Wilkinson, Ray Henderson, Ken Houghton, Mick Milner, Chris Simpkin, Dennis Butler.

them, catch them!" Quick as a flash Ian shouted back: "What do you want for twenty-eight quid a week – fucking Yashin?"'

Although the Russian international goalkeeper Lev Yashin had a fabulous reputation, in reality he was probably earning peanuts in his own country! Interestingly, the wages of Hull City players in the 1970s seem paltry in relation to the fabulous money on offer thirty years later. Although nowadays a player of Wagstaff's class and reputation would almost certainly be earning tens of thousands a year, with the prospect of becoming a millionaire not too wild an expectation, in those days the average salary would be pitiful in comparison. Ken is philosophical about the inflated salaries for today's top stars. For him the money was important, but his love of the game was the most powerful driving force. He recalls: 'The wage included bonuses for a winning run, goals scored and other incentives. Funnily enough, within that, the win bonus was just £4! It was half that for a draw! When I first arrived at Hull City, I said to Chillo, "What are the bonuses like here?" He replied, "I dunno, I've only been here four years!" Once, one of the lads went in to see Cliff about pay. He was in there for about three hours. The pay request just went in one ear and out the other. Cliff just waffled on about tactics using a board on his desk and a load of tiddlywinks!'

After friendly matches against Hibernian and Sunderland, the Tigers kicked off the 1966/67 season with successive away defeats at Coventry and Lincoln (Football League Cup) and failed to score in either game. On 27 August, in front of 20,438 spectators at Boothferry Park, they registered their first League win of the season against Bury. Wagstaff scored twice. City's defence was shaky at times in a generally drab game illuminated by flashes of Wagstaff brilliance and characterised by some extremely robust tackling. (This included a chop on Waggy by centre forward George Kerr at a time when it looked like the forward would register his first hat-trick in Division Two.)

Already, goals in the 29th and 89th minute had once more demonstrated Waggy's ice-cool finishing. It was yet another example of his ability to pop up at any time in the game and put the ball in the net.

Waggy shared the goal tally with Ken Houghton in the side's 2-0 away win at Norwich on 31 August. Each of the three goals scored so far in the first three games of the season had involved beating defenders, losing them with his speed – and then shooting coolly past an advancing 'keeper. It was a practised art form that never lost its appeal for a growing band of admirers. Looking back, Ken was keen to acknowledge the role of

The Partnership: Chilton hammers the ball goalwards with Wagstaff moving into position to collect the pass or any rebound from the goalkeeper.

The two Kens: Ken Wagstaff and Ken Houghton train for a visit to Rotherham.

Inside forward Ray Henderson receives a benefit cheque from chairman Harold Needler. Looking on are, from left to right, Dennis Butler, Alan Jarvis, Ian McKechnie, Chris Simpkin, Ian Butler and Ken Wagstaff.

others: 'In the two games against Bury and Norwich at the start of the season, Ken Houghton's play was superb. He helped lay on the chances. Mick Milner and Chris Simpkin played brilliantly at the back.'

After the game at Norwich it was to be another five matches before Waggy would find the net again. However, his goal at home in the 5-0 humbling of the Canaries in the return game at Boothferry Park was the first of nine in a five-game spell that saw the Tigers record four wins and a defeat. This included a 6-1 annihilation of Northampton Town on 23 September in which Waggy and Chris Chilton scored twice. Butler and Henderson shared the spoils, each with brilliantly taken goals to their credit.

The first of those goals was testimony to the player's coolness, resilience and abject skill. Having received the ball in the inside-right position, he was faced with drawing the ball away from the defender and a harrying 'keeper. Having beaten both of them, the task of scoring seemed impossible given the narrowness of the angle. The fact that the ball ended up in the net, speaks volumes for his speed of reaction, general awareness and scoring accuracy. A cartoon in the next club programme showed a striker, with a tiger's head, scoring, with the caption 'Clickety clix – that makes it six!' It proudly proclaimed that the Tigers had 'soled and heeled the cobblers'.

On the eve of the Northampton game, the Division Two table showed the Tigers in second place – a point behind Bolton Wanderers, but having played a game more than all of their immediate rivals. It made fabulous reading.

CITY v. NORTHAMPTON. Goal No. 4 for City as Chris Chilton puts in a powerful shot to beat keeper Harvey

Cartoon in the Hull City programme for the match following the Tigers' 6-1 victory over Northampton Town on 23 September 1966.

Division Two: 22 September 1966

	P	W	D	L	F	A	Pts
1 Bolton	8	6	1	1	18	8	13
2 HULL CITY	9	6	0	3	20	8	12
3 Crystal Palace	8	5	2	1	15	10	12
4 Ipswich	8	5	1	2	16	9	11
5 Blackburn	8	5	1	2	14	12	11
6 Coventry	8	4	2	2	9	7	10

Pre-season photograph, Hull City first team, reserves and juniors. From left to right, back row: Billy Brown, Don Beardsley, Dave Lill, Ian McKechnie, Barry White, Norman Lees, Stuart Blampey, Roger De Vries. Second row: Andy Davidson (coaching staff), Alec Martin, Dennis Butler Frank Banks, Paddy Greenwood, Geoff Barker, Tom Wilson, Chris Simpkin, Paul O'Riley, Ray Pettit, Stuart Pearson, John McSeveney (coaching staff), Jimmy Lodge (masseur). Third row: Malcolm Lord, Alan Jarvis, Ken Houghton, Ken Wagstaff, Chris Chilton, Billy Wilkinson, Ian Butler, Rob Smith. Front row: Bobby Smith, Roy Greenwood, Stephen Gregson, David Spencer, Stephen Holbrook, Melvin Green, Barry McCunnell.

After the match, local sports reporter Brian Taylor recorded that: 'For consistency and overall dominance this was perhaps the finest display the side have turned in since manager Cliff Britton gathered together the forward line which is now the envy of most managers in the country.'

Now in the Division Two spotlight, Waggy's performances were yet again attracting interest from top clubs. Millionaire chairman Harold Needler had allegedly taken calls from interested parties and told them bluntly: 'You've got more chance of getting the town hall clock.' From the player's point of view, he was enjoying his football: 'It was great time at Hull City. Chris and I were big mates and we were supported by a brilliant team of players. I did want to play in Division One, but hoped that could be achieved with Hull City. As it happens, the contractual situation with players was in favour of clubs in those days. They decided if they were going to sell you.'

Five days later, the Tigers beat Portsmouth 2-0 at Boothferry Park, with goals from Houghton and Wagstaff. It put the Tigers in the top spot in Division Two. Chairman Harold Needler was on business in New York. Officials telephoned him with the news. At home, Waggy revealed his feelings in the local press: 'You wait until the heavy

1966 clash with Oxford United. Ken Wagstaff heads for goal with winger Ian Butler looking on.

grounds come. Those are what we are really waiting for.' Earlier defeats had been on hard pitches. Clearly he felt their chances would improve on soft surfaces. He also pointed out the fact that five of the opening games, including the Football League Cup defeat at Lincoln, had been away from home.

Looking back years later, he talked about how it was to play in Division Two: 'In some ways it was easier than in the Third. Division Two defenders marked you. In the Third they marked you and kicked you at the same time. I found a little more space to play in, but on the other hand there was a little more finesse in that the defenders waited a fraction of a second longer to see what I was going to do.'

There was no doubt that opponents feared the City front line. The depth of talent was so great that the combined strike force took some holding: 'In the previous season, I'd scored 27 goals, Chillo had got 25 and Ken Houghton 22 goals. Leaving that aside, we had two free-scoring wingers in Ian Butler and Ray Henderson who scored 26 between them! On top of that were goals in the Cup.'

The press found themselves struggling to find enough superlatives to describe the success being enjoyed by the Tigers. However, in sounding ominous warnings about weaknesses in defence, they were making public what was already concerning many on

Hull City *v.* Oxford United, 1966: Waggy shoots.

the terraces. No less a critic was Raich Carter who, in an interview with reporter Edgar Turner, called for large-scale spending to guarantee what he felt would otherwise be a precarious assault on Division One. He said: 'This is the time for Hull to drive for success. This is the time to spend again, the time to sign at least two more players. For with this golden opportunity it's not just enough to hope for promotion. It is time to make certain of it. Not only that, it is just not enough to enjoy a place in Division One. No less than the top and with it European football must be the aim. Hull City can be the best, the most-respected club in Yorkshire, maybe among the best in the land. I know all about Leeds. After all, I managed them as I once did Hull City. But I was in Boothferry's previous great days, when we had the biggest crowds in the club's history. I want that and more for my old club now.'

Raich went on to point out the lessons given by the two Merseyside clubs. He cited Everton's £110,000 purchase of Alan Ball following their Cup win and Bill Shankly's signing of full-back Bob McNab – despite having already won the Championship. Not for the first time, Carter's words were prophetic.

Of the first 13 games of the season, the Tigers had won nine – including five wins in a six-game sequence. They had scored 30 goals with only 14 against and had managed

Hull City *v.* Mansfield Town, 1966. Waggy heads the Tigers into the lead.

six winning home matches in a row. In a 4-2 away win at Cardiff on 8 October 1966 Waggy scored all four goals, making him Division Two's top goalscorer. The four-goal blast was the third in his Football League career – once for each of the divisions in which he has played. He was also one of the leading goalscorers in the entire Football League. His League and cup career total was now 174 goals in 293 appearances.

The press were full of praise for the twenty-three year old and Roger Malone noted: 'I often wonder why England have never used him. Maybe his time will be the next World Cup, Mexico 1970.'

With Waggy having scored in the 7th and 12th minutes at Cardiff, a band of City supporters had already begun a 'massacre, massacre' chant. Cardiff fought back and two goals in eight minutes saw them level again. However, a characteristically powerful kick from 'keeper McKechnie found Wagstaff, who raced clear. With the greatest composure, he beat the 'keeper to register a hat-trick.

The final goal in the 88th minute typified another facet of Waggy's play. Chilton had cracked in a low drive of such power that the 'keeper had his work cut out to keep the ball out. The rebound fell to a lurking Wagstaff, exactly in the right spot to deliver the final killer blow into the net.

Winger Ian Butler beats former England international full-back Jimmy Armfield of Blackpool to cross the ball on 2 September 1967.

Such was the quality of the Hull City performance on that day that the Welsh supporters in a gate of 10,000 were moved to applaud the moves that led to the goals. Despite the scoreline, the game had not entirely been one way. But for a series of superlative saves by McKechnie, the margin would have been less flattering.

On 15 October 1966, the Tigers played Wolverhampton Wanderers. In a game that featured goals from Chilton, Henderson and Butler, it was Ken Wagstaff that earned the praise from a national media still baying for his inclusion in the England squad. Alan Thompson wrote: 'One of the forwards in our next World Cup side could well be Ken Wagstaff. Years ago when he played for Mansfield, I wrote that "this lad will one day play for England". And I alter that opinion only slightly. He MUST play for England. Twelve goals already this season underline his appetite for scoring, but he is also completely unselfish. Twice he chose to pass to better-placed colleagues when he might have grabbed the glory. The first led to Hull's opening goal, while the second, when he tried to give Chris Chilton an open goal though he himself had only goalkeeper Fred Davis to beat, was well intercepted.' The reporter waxed lyrical about the brand of football being played by the Tigers under the headline: 'No Stopping This Side'. He went on to say: 'The best football in the North and possibly the country is being played by Hull City.

Everyone should be made to see them – theorists who believe that victory stems from defence, method men who preach 'one man, one job', and most of all those who crave for excitement. Hull are the mystics of soccer – throwbacks who believe in all-out attack and who therefore excite. Soccer for them is a matter of shooting and scoring – not a game of chess.'

After the Wolves game, City inexplicably suffered five League defeats in a row. Things improved a little in the run up to Christmas with draws against Charlton Athletic and Coventry City. Sandwiched in between, were wins against Derby County (3-2) and Crystal Palace (6-1). Waggy scored in each of the victories, but his contribution was marked by his team play in helping to create chances for the others.

In the 3-2 victory at Derby on 3 December, Waggy had a hand in Billy Wilkinson's first goal as he beat one defender and slid the ball through for his team-mate to score. Wilkinson's second goal was a brilliant individual effort through the middle. Finally, Waggy made sure of the points as he drifted past two defenders and chipped the ball into the net past a helpless 'keeper.

In the 20 League games from and including Boxing Day until the end of the season, the Tigers managed only five victories. With five draws and 10 defeats recorded, their form was disappointing to say the least. Even allowing for three games missed, Waggy had found the net only four times, with strike partner Chris Chilton having notched up only two more. The picture is even clearer when it is revealed that the last 11 games included seven defeats – 11 goals scored and 26 conceded.

The Tigers lost 3-2 at Bury on 31 December 1966. Although Waggy had scored in the 35th minute, the Tigers went into the interval 3-1 down. During the second half, a ball from Paddy Greenwood found Billy Wilkinson. In the subsequent interchange involving Chilton, Wagstaff collided with the Bury 'keeper and fell headlong into the goal. Eventually, Harker picked Waggy up as play went on and took him to trainer Gus Mclean waiting on the touchline. At first, a broken leg was suspected and Waggy found himself in the local hospital: 'Judging by the pain, it looked as if it was a break, but luckily the x-rays showed it was just severe bruising. I was out for the next game but that was all.'

That season, things were little better in the FA Cup. Against third-round opponents Portsmouth, the Tigers went down 1-3 on neutral territory after drawing in the previous two games. Although City had been beaten 2-1 in a February home friendly against Slovan Bratislava, at least Waggy had some personal consolation from finding the net against top European opposition.

One notable debut in March 1967 was that of Malcolm Lord – possibly one of the most under-appreciated players at the club. His professional, workmanlike and athletic performances were like a catalyst in the team's engine room. He seemed almost invisible to praise, yet vulnerable to carping criticism when things went wrong. His play was solid and supportive to colleagues making him a key player in the squad. Waggy recalls: 'Mally Lord would run all day for us. He was a great asset to the team. Due to his style, when he played well, people hardly noticed he was there. He made it easier for the rest of us to perform.'

In a term that had promised so much, the Tigers completed the season in disap-pointing style. However, in his 39 League appearances, Waggy had scored 21 goals. The partnership with Chris Chilton had yielded a joint total of 38 League goals. Now in a higher division, they were still highly effective.

Attendances at Boothferry Park, having been gradually built up in the early season peaked at 35,630 in the Boxing Day match against Huddersfield Town. Waggy had scored in that 2-0 victory. He recalls the terrific atmosphere in the ground on that day and his feelings after scoring: 'There were many big games at Boothferry Park with big gates over 20,000. You could feel the excitement and the electricity. Obviously, for a ground that size, 35,000 is a terrific attendance. Big gates never bothered me. I just got on with it. You can't lose concentration on the game.

'Scoring always gives me a big kick. People ask me about it regularly – about how it feels when I see the ball go in. I tell them that I never look. I kick the ball – or very, very rarely I might head it in. At the moment it's on its way I just turn away and that's it. I don't look any more. Mostly, I just close my eyes and run back for the restart.'

There are instances when Waggy's humour got in the way of this normal practice after the team scored. In one game on a snow-covered pitch he was seen to chat with the 'keeper who had just let in a goal after failing to meet a cross. The 'keeper was sitting disconsolate in the snow when Waggy uttered a few words of encouragement. Immediately afterwards, the 'keeper scooped up a hand full of snow and hurled it at a sniggering Waggy. When asked to explain the 'keeper's reaction Waggy chuckled: 'I just told him he was fucking useless and that he should have caught it!'

8
Marking Time 1967–1970

The 1967/68 season began by keeping up the previous year's habit of opening the pre-season friendly matches against Scottish opposition. In front of a gate of 11,665, the Tigers took on Hearts at Boothferry Park. Waggy carried on his tradition of scoring against Scottish opposition but this time doubled last year's tally with two well-taken strikes. Chillo and Ian Butler also announced their intentions for the new season with a goal each. Sunderland were less easy opponents and the sides shared the spoils in a six-goal encounter which drew just under 3,000 fewer supporters.

Carlisle United provided first blood for the new League campaign with just over 19,000 fans taking up the cause for what was hoped would be promotion that year. However, away games at Bolton Wanderers and Blackburn Rovers set a dismal trend with the Tigers going down 6-1 and 2-0 respectively. Bolton came to Boothferry Park on 30 August and took the points and with them the satisfaction of doing an early double – having scored eight with only two in reply.

From left to right, back row: Terry Heath, Mike Brown, Mike Milner, Maurice Swan, Norman Corner, Les Collinson, Billy Wilkinson. Front row: Alan Jarvis, Ray Henderson, Ken Wagstaff, Chris Chilton, Andy Davidson (capt.), Ken Houghton, Ron Young, Chris Simpkin, Dennis Butler.

Within 48 hours Blackpool sent almost 17,000 Tigers' fans home miserable at their fourth defeat in a row – this time by a single goal. Two days later, the Tigers raided the St Andrews ground of Birmingham in the hope of rescuing their pride – or at least some points. The Luftwaffe had scored 20 direct hits on the ground in the war years but went home frustrated. It was no different for the Tigers who found themselves on the receiving end of a six-goal blitz from the Blues. At least Waggy and Chillo had the satisfaction of at least opening their League accounts with a goal apiece.

A pair of draws, as the comedian might say, did then bring some comfort, with Waggy netting against Millwall, if not against Crystal Palace. Queens Park Rangers helped ease his goal drought in a Football League Cup game that saw the Tigers make an early exit by the odd goal with 8 games gone. It was turning out to be a dour season, with the defence leaking 19 goals in the League and only seven being scored at the other end. Worryingly, in two of the defeats, six goals had been conceded in each game.

By the time Middlesbrough came to Boothferry Park on 23 September, fans were hardly surprised to see their team beaten 2-0. However, they managed a draw against Bristol City with a goal from Chilton and a pair from Houghton. Had the tide of despair been halted?

The 'Chillo And Waggy' act was on stage once more at Preston, but the home side managed to score just one more. It was City's 10th game without a win. Out of the six League games away from home so far, that had been the fourth defeat – with nine goals for and 21 scored against. With only a single home win to date on the opening game of the season, the five Boothferry Park matches had also returned three defeats. Remarkably, the goal tally was just three in favour and twice as many against. The writing seemed to be on the wall for what appeared to be a shaky defensive set up. But what had happened to the fabled strike force?

The answer came in the very next game as Houghton and Wagstaff helped sink Queens Park Rangers. A week later Plymouth fell victims to a 5-2 defeat with Houghton, Chilton, Wagstaff, Simpkin and Ron Young scoring. Young had been with the Tigers since August 1983. In his few performances, he'd rarely disappointed. Despite some optimism, it all turned sour with consecutive defeats to Cardiff, Portsmouth and Norwich City. Only Wagstaff's strike at Cardiff countered the seven-goal tally against in that period.

New signing Tom Wilson made his debut against the Canaries on 11 November. The Millwall player, who had become revered following consecutive promotions, had been snatched from under the noses of Manchester City and Arsenal. It seemed that the manager was now trying to get a grip of the defensive issues that had perhaps prevented a successive promotion bid in the previous year.

Almost symmetrically, the following trio of matches were all wins against Aston Villa, Derby County and Rotherham United – all three teams featuring in the bottom seven teams in the division at the end of the season.

After having played in only three of the earlier League matches, Ian McKechnie returned in goal against Villa and was ever-present for the rest of the season. The match also marked the end of Andy Davidson's long and distinguished League career. Shortly afterwards, Frank Banks moved permanently into a defensive slot.

Waggy (left) in pre-season training July 1969.

Up front, it was pretty much business as usual, with Waggy, Ian Butler, Houghton and Chilton remaining in place. Ray Henderson was around most of the time from mid-November onwards having been missing for the early part of the season.

Following the earlier results, it seemed the plot now called for three draws – and the Tigers duly obliged with successive 1-1 results against Charlton, Carlisle and Blackburn.

Only an Ian Butler goal in the last match spoiled Waggy's claim to a goal in each of those games. It seemed that the changes had taken some effect.

However, Huddersfield Town dented the notion that things were under control, by handing out a two-goal lesson on Boxing Day. Four days later, the Tigers held them to a 1-1 draw at Boothferry Park. As New Year was celebrated, only a great optimist would have predicted promotion that year. In fact, he'd probably have been sectioned for such thoughts.

Now being showcased against top clubs, there remained considerable interest in Waggy. Almost completely, he was kept in the dark about such activity: 'I'd heard rumours that some of the top Division One clubs wanted to sign me but I was never told officially. It was different in those days. The club had all the options and the players were only told what the clubs wanted them to be told. It was my ambition to play at the highest level. My dream would have been to play for Manchester United. Given the opportunity I may have gone but the fans were great to me at Boothferry Park. Obviously, I would have loved to have played in Division One with Hull City. Throughout my time with them, it always remained my hope and my aim.

In the Huddersfield game at Boothferry Park, the Tigers had netted only once. It was to be the same outcome in the next four League games with the goals coming in that period from Wagstaff, Chilton (2) and Young. With only a single victory and a draw to show from that spell, the season was already all but over. However, the FA Cup offered the prospect of injecting some spark into the otherwise dismal outlook. Despite the mediocre season so far, there was still faith in the prospect of building on the core of talent many felt could still operate at a higher level. In recent years, the club's cup record had provided great excitement and hope.

In a twelve-day spell from 31 January, City played Middlesbrough four times – three times in the FA Cup. Following a 1-1 away draw featuring a goal from Chris Chilton, Waggy grabbed both goals in a 2-2 replay at Boothferry Park in front of 33,916 fans. It demonstrated yet again that the club had a potentially massive fan base. The passion was there on the terraces. The Tigers went out 1-0 in the second replay but not before Boro had signalled their intentions by defeating the Tigers 2-1 at home in the League – a game Waggy missed through injury.

The home game against Bristol City on 10 February 1968 was a classic. It provided a much needed morale boost. The Tigers struggled in the first half against an almost impenetrable Bristol defence. A John Galley header in the 33rd minute had put the visitors ahead. Yet, within nine minutes of the restart Waggy had destroyed them with three finely taken goals. In fact, the game had gone so badly in the first half, he had decided to revert to a central attacking role: 'In the season up until then, I'd been asked to move out to the wings and drag the heavy marking with me to leave a gap in the centre. It didn't work in the Bristol City game so I just decided to go out and play my old game. Luckily, the boss didn't complain after it ended up in a hat-trick!'

The rout began in the 50th minute when Chilton rose above the defence to nod the ball down. Like rabbits in a car's headlights, the defence hesitated momentarily. In a flash, Waggy was on the ball. Turning quickly, he lashed it into the net. Within the space of a minute, Butler had netted a second from a crossed ball. Two minutes later, Waggy fastened on to a Chris Simpkin header forward. With his back to the goal, he scored with a spectacular overhead kick. Finally, a through ball from the inventive Ken Houghton found Wagstaff yet again. Despite a challenge from Terry Bush, Waggy bustled onward to lash a low ball into the net past the advancing Gibson. Although Bristol pulled one back, the 4-2 victory eased the Tigers' precarious League position.

In the remaining 13 games of the season, the Tigers won four, drew five and lost four games, finishing 17th – six places from the bottom. That season, having scored 58 goals, they had a worrying 73 scored against them. It was a rate of 1.74 conceded per game. In fact the season's averages mask the fact that the rate was much higher at the start of the season before adjustments were made to the side. Up until the Aston Villa game on 18 November, the rate was 2.23 goals per game conceded.

Thereafter it dropped to 1.4 goals per game conceded – comparable to the performance in the promotion year when the comparable statistic was 1.34. Ipswich Town, the champions in that year had returned a season's rate of 1.04 – 29 goals fewer conceded. They had also scored 21 more goals with a scoring ratio of 1.89 per game compared with City's strike rate of 1.38 goals per game.

'Had we made some new signings at the back the previous year I think we'd have made the First Division,' says Waggy. 'Cliff kept faith in the hope that it would all come together. We scored plenty of goals against better opposition in the first season after going up but we let too many in as well. In 1967/68, we found it more difficult to perform at the front because the service was affected to some extent by the problems at the back and to some degree by the better quality opposition.'

Goals scored, not taking account of the two seasons in Division Two where four games less are played, had dropped from 109 in the promotion season to 77 in the next term, finally resting on 58 goals in 1967/68. While these statistics make interesting reading, League position is decided only by points taken, except in the event of teams being equal on points when goal difference counts.

A high-scoring defeat and a low-scoring defeat both yield no points. Sides can grind out results and gain promotion or they can be free-scoring and still succeed – providing they gain wins from conceding less. Although the information is blindingly obvious, the statistics give some insight into the issues arising for Hull City at that time. In the final analysis however, there are many factors to take into account.

In late summer 1968, the now traditional pre-season friendly against Scottish opposition was far from a piece of cake as Dundee edged a 1-0 win. It was hardly a surprise when Liverpool came to Boothferry Park in search of the expected victory. That they scored five was unexpected, but at least Wagstaff, Chilton and Houghton extracted morale-boosting goals.

On Sunday 1 September, Ken swapped his football boots for a cricket bat in a charity game against a Lords Taverners side that included Brian Rix, Ian Carmichael, Leslie Crowther and Jim Laker. A Welton Invitation XI comprised Ken Wagstaff, Chris Chilton, Ken Houghton and several Hull rugby players, including David Doyle Davidson and John Whitley.

When it came to the first day of the season at Blackpool, the Tigers were in little mood for a visit to the illuminations after their 2-0 afternoon defeat. Blackburn added

Enjoying training: Dennis Butler and Ken Wagstaff.

The face of football! Ken Wagstaff pictured on the ball.

to the gloom by winning at Boothferry Park a week later in front of a dismal crowd of 13,345. Only two years earlier, average gates had been almost double that level. In a climate of financial austerity reports in the press suggested that Britton could now be prepared to sell Chilton, Wagstaff and Houghton. Waggy missed the next game at Fulham with a knee injury.

In the next seven League matches after the Blackburn game, the Tigers registered six draws – conceding only 6 goals. Like a jewel, shining in the middle of this run was a 3-0 win against Middlesbrough – the culmination of a three-match Wagstaff run of a goal a game.

Chilton and Butler were also finding the net and in the absence of high scoring, the team were grinding out results. It seemed the messages from the previous two seasons had at least been read. With Don Beardsley now firmly in a defensive role things were looking brighter.

'It was obvious we needed to tighten up at the back,' says Waggy. 'We were facing good teams and with opportunities to score being few and far between, games could hang on the odd goal. When the chances came we took them. The secret was to keep the opposition out without being boring and negative.'

The point was made precisely in the match against a robust Bolton Wanderers side, where Wagstaff scored the only goal of the game to bag the points. Up until that point, the match had 'draw' written all over it. However, in the 70th minute Chilton won the ball in the City half and threaded it through to Waggy who was in full flight.

The referee waved play on as Hatton tried to handle the ball in a desperate attempt to frustrate the charge forward. Having sidestepped the Bolton defence, Waggy then sent a drive coolly past the advancing Hopkinson. Shortly afterwards he resisted harrying Bolton defenders and repaid the earlier compliment with a pass to Chilton but the centre forward hit the side netting.

The press reported that an offer of £50,000 for Wagstaff from Huddersfield had been turned down by manager Cliff Britton, who remained convinced that the side could win promotion once the rearguard had settled.

A week later, Ken Houghton was the hat-trick hero in a 3-2 victory at Millwall. Norwich, Derby County and Huddersfield all fell victim in what added up to a purple spell of five wins in a row with only three goals conceded. Although Preston spoiled the party, it was only by a single goal.

In the earlier home game against Huddersfield, which City won 3-0 to take their run at that point to 12 League games without defeat, one press report emphasised the cheeky element of Wagstaff's game. It read: 'WAGGY, DIRECTOR, PRODUCER, STAR. They laughed at Boothferry Park yesterday as Wagstaff, their arrogant impresario, treated them to an exhibition of head and feet juggling…like in a training session…with the opposing defence flat-footed spectators…and then with his special brand of alchemy, he appeared in the penalty area to blast the ball home.'

Against Cardiff City on 26 October, Waggy scored a hat-trick in a six-goal thriller. Soon afterwards, Carlisle repeated the message about how to take full points by scoring only one goal. However, Waggy had a different script for the next game and slotted in two goals in the side's 3-0 defeat of Bury, with Tom Wilson netting the third.

City went into the game against Carlisle with aspirations of topping the table, but the 1-0 defeat was a setback and was due, for a change, to below-par finishing. The headline in one paper read: 'Wagstaff miss proves costly'. It had been extremely difficult to prise open the defence and perhaps the only real chance of the match for the Tigers had fallen to Waggy who had shot high with only the 'keeper to beat. It was a rare, but costly miss as Carlisle went ahead shortly afterwards: 'We did manage to get a few shots in on goal, but they were all blocked. Sometimes it's fair to say that a chance falls to you and it goes wrong. That's life. You just have to get on with it and make sure the next one goes in. I never dwelt on the odd miss.'

Chris Simpkin underlined the point: 'Great strikers never let the odd miss worry them. They just get on with looking to stick away the next chance.'

Certainly, Waggy's career record and reputation speaks for itself. His coolness in front of goal and his long-term reliability have never seriously been in question. Where sometimes players would suffer a loss of confidence, Waggy's temperament allowed him to just carry on doing the business. That resilience was a characteristic of his and one of the reasons that made him different.

The 3-0 home win against Bury included two for Wagstaff – one short of his 100th goal for City. More grinding draws followed against Charlton and Portsmouth, with Waggy taking another goal-a-game run to three games. In the last five games he had scored seven goals. However, a 5-2 defeat at Birmingham City was a worrying reversal of fortune. It was not championship form, but there did seem to be a better grip in defence. Attendances at Boothferry Park were holding up, but only big name sides, a Cup run, or winning consistency in the League would bring in the big gates.

December started well with two wins against Crystal Palace and Huddersfield. Waggy netted in the side's 1-1 draw at Preston. So far that month, six goals had been scored with only one in reply. Pleasingly, Chilton had scored three with Butler and Wagstaff keeping their names to the fore with goals apiece. On the scoresheet at Huddersfield was local boy David Lill from Albrough.

It was a bleak Christmas and New Year, as the Tigers crashed to three defeats in a row – this time conceding six goals and scoring only one in return. The game against Norwich marked Chillo's last League appearance of the season through injury. The lay off artificially depleted his season's goals tally to just five from 22 League appearances.

Waggy missed mid-January's goal-less draw at Bury but bounced back to score in the 5-1 home victory against Charlton Athletic. More defeats followed at Portsmouth and Crystal Palace. Little wonder then that the supporters were calling the Tigers a 'yo-yo' team.

Attendances at Boothferry Park were slipping as mid-table mediocrity beckoned. As if by tradition, three yawning draws emerged from the proceedings in the first three weeks of March. Echoes of championship euphoria were now just a murmur, but the sight of the heroes on the field of play was ever the eternal flame of hope.

For the remaining eight League games of the season, the Tigers trudged to 11th place down a path of three wins, two draws and three defeats. The lowest home League attendance of the season on 15 April saw the Tigers lose 2-1 to Birmingham City. On a brighter note over the last five matches, Waggy had scored five times, including a hat-

Ken Wagstaff.

trick in the 4-0 defeat of Fulham, who were admittedly the club that finished bottom on 25 points.

The season saw a slight improvement on the previous term's League position. Unfortunately, the FA Cup had not provided any consolation this time, with the Tigers having gone out at the first time of asking to Wolves on 4 January. The fact that 27,526 fans turned up was testimony to the Cup's drawing power.

It was an indifferent season in terms of reaching the success everyone craved. Ken understood and appreciated what the fans were going through. He also acknowledges the part his team-mates had played: 'We always had great support at Boothferry Park. The fans were fantastic. In Division Three, when we were scoring lots and lots of goals, they lapped it up. It was exciting, dramatic football. The noise encouraged us no end. Scoring was brilliant. Obviously, it's satisfying to do your job and put the ball in the net or to make a goal for someone else. But knowing that you'd made thousands of people happy was something else.

'I know that the people of Hull thought the world of me, Chillo and the others, but we knew they were there every week and we wanted to do it for them as well as ourselves. The press tended to blow up the publicity for the goalscorers and that's to be expected I suppose – but success is really a team effort.

'Chillo's goals were fantastic. You only have to look at the video footage. He was brilliant in the air – an exceptional talent. He gave me first-class service and I tried to do the same for him. Chillo could score equally well with his feet, often scoring amazing goals, sometimes at long range.

'He also helped distract the defenders away from the rest of us. It was part of the plan. Once at training we heard this "wooo wooo" sound. Everyone looked round and it was Chillo. When asked what he was up to, he simply said that he was practising being a decoy.

'Ken Houghton scored some brilliant goals – along with Ian Butler, John McSeveney and the others. After going up, Division Two was a tougher nut to crack. Gradually, we consolidated and made a few changes but it was slow to take effect. All we could do as forwards was to go out there and play the game the manager decided and take the chances that came along. At times, it was frustrating for everyone, but we kept plugging away.' Waggy made 39 League appearances that season and scored 20 goals.

Kilmarnock provided the customary Scottish flavour to 1969/70 pre-season matches. Chillo announced his presence with two well-taken goals in the draw that preceded a sweet 1-0 victory over Newcastle United.

The season kicked off at Queens Park Rangers. It wasn't the brightest of starts – a 3-0 defeat. After home victories against Norwich and Bristol City, the Tigers served up a pair of away defeats. Thereafter, just over 12,000 turned up at Boothferry Park to see a goal-less draw against Birmingham City and the scene appeared set for yet another season of mid-table mediocrity.

Local lad Stuart Blampey had made his debut in the Norwich home game. A versatile player, he graced seven different positions. In his first season, Stuart played on the right wing and managed to get his name on the scoresheet alongside Chris Chilton in the next home game against Bristol City.

In a Boothferry Park encounter on 29 August, Chris Simpkin broke the deadlock against Blackpool with a well-taken goal. It was to be a successful season for the visitors. They were promoted in second place but enjoyed only a single season in Division One. Ian Butler netted at Carlisle a week later. Unfortunately, they scored one more goal than the Tigers. So far, with eight games of the season gone, Waggy still had to find the net.

Although Ian Butler had managed three goals, Chris Chilton was also into a lean spell, having scored just one League goal, in the home game against Bristol City. In the next three League games the Tigers scored a total of ten goals. Chillo and Waggy had scored six between them. Although the two victories had raised hopes that things were looking brighter, a defeat at Villa Park was made even more worrying as Waggy sustained an injury that led to him missing the next three matches.

After a 1-1 home draw against Charlton Athletic, the following two games put things into perspective. The away defeats at Sheffield United and Bristol had yielded only one Chilton goal against six conceded. Waggy's return for the next game against Oxford coincided with the first of two Chilton absences. However, goals from Wilkinson, Simpkin and Barker saw off Oxford United in front of 8,136 supporters at Boothferry Park.

After missing the next game, Waggy was ever present for the rest of the season. Throughout the entire League programme, Ken Houghton missed only one League match. Ian Butler missed three games and Chilton only six. Minor injury problems aside, consistency in terms of matches played for the forward positions was good.

On the other hand, switches in midfield and defence – forced or otherwise – conspired to deny the side the necessary consistency and understandings required to maximize the considerable firepower available on the front line. There were question marks over competence and some felt that the changes being made were simply akin to shuffling the deck chairs on the *Titanic*.

If defeats against Swindon and Huddersfield weren't enough warning, the 6-0 drubbing at Cardiff City on 1 November set alarm bells ringing big time. Yet Cliff Britton remained at the helm. It was the fourth season of football in Division Two. The club had expressed a burning ambition to reach Division One. Britton had delivered only mid-table mediocrity. In Division Two, critics implored him to strengthen the central defence. It was a long-standing cry. Although it had been answered in some measure, results were less than satisfactory.

Hull City were conceding an average of 1.83 goals per game. Throughout their campaign, Preston North End, who were to be relegated that year, let in goals at an average of 1.5 goals per game. The comparison is chilling. Although the Tigers would improve that attrition rate by the end of the season, Britton's days were numbered.

On 8 November 1969, Preston North End provided the fodder for a most welcome 3-1 victory. It seemed like old times, with the Chillo and Waggy double-act firing on all cylinders, and into the net. A week later, the trip to Middlesbrough brought everyone back down to earth but only on the back of a single goal. In an eight-game spell up to the end of January 1970, the Tigers won three matches, lost three and drew two.

Seventeen goals were scored with Waggy scoring six and Chilton five. Ken Houghton, Ian Butler and Chris Simpkin also found the net. Attendances grew to 15,551 for the

31 January Yorkshire derby game against Sheffield United. However, despite a two-goal burst by Waggy the crowd went home disappointed after their team was beaten 3-2. That year, the FA Cup held little interest for the Tigers after they went down 1-0 to Manchester City at Maine Road on 3 January.

Aside from two reversals to Queens Park Rangers and Millwall, the Tigers would go unbeaten in the League for the rest of the season. The rate of goals conceded dropped to an average of 1.5 per game. Importantly, the side scored at an average rate of 2 goals per game. Although those statistics are crude measures of performance, they do provide some insight into what was happening. In the last 14 games of the season, the Tigers drew seven, won five and lost only two games. Possibly due to a little more consistency at the back, at least they were holding their own.

The last game of the season marked the debut of Stuart Pearson at centre forward in place of Chris Chilton. It was a cameo appearance, but in due course the strong, fast-moving player would make his mark in a more permanent way. Pearson had arrived at the club in May 1966 from local junior football. Although his scoring rate never approached that of the great Chillo, he did have determination and strength in good measure. Ken recalls that: 'Stuart grew up with Chillo and me at City. He watched us play and trained with us. Eventually he got into the first team. He was extremely quick off the mark for a well-built lad. That burst of pace gave him a few problems with Achilles injuries but it didn't stop him finally breaking through and then going on to make a mark with Manchester United and England.'

Waggy's goal tally that year totalled 18 in 38 League appearances. He'd scored a further goal against Norwich City in the Football League Cup win back in September. However, Derby County organised City's early exit in the third round.

Goalkeeper Ian Mckechnie had been ever present throughout the season. Having picked the ball out of the net 70 times that season, it had been a little more exercise than the year before when the ball flew past him on 18 fewer occasions. At the other end, the Tigers had scored 72 goals compared to 59 the previous year. Despite the higher strike rate, the Tigers had won a point less in the League having finished 13th compared to 11th in 1968/69.

It was an unlucky number for manager Cliff Britton. He left the club on May 1970. Although he could take great satisfaction from having created that wonderful promotion-winning side that had at least secured a mid-table foothold in Division Two, he'd clearly taken the club as far as he was able.

Mick Brown played for Hull City in the Britton era. Now the head scout at Manchester United, his words encapsulated the general feeling of all the players at the time: 'Cliff Britton was a man ahead of his time. He was exceptionally meticulous, very thoughtful and well respected by everyone. Nobody had a bad word about him. He was a disciplinarian, but had the brains to be able to manage off-the-field activities. Players liked a drink, but never before a game. He found the balance. He was very committed to the team's success and was often physically sick with tension just before games.'

Former City midfielder Chris Simpkin endorses that view and emphasises the exceptional level of organisation: 'As players, we knew exactly what our job was. I was really in to football at the time and knew about almost every team in the country, including

Hull City's Chris Simpkin.

Ken Wagstaff in August 1970.

24 October 1970, Hull City v Sheffield United: Top-drawer goal as Waggy beats two United defenders before sending class goalkeeper Alan Hodgkinson the wrong way.

the individual players. Cliff would often ask me to speak at the team talks before a game. He organised everything at the club, not just the team.'

Despite, not delivering Division One football in the city, the Britton era lives on in the hearts of City fans as a period characterised by scintillating and pulsating goal-mouth action laced with wonderful memories of Chillo, Waggy and the other perhaps lesser-sung, but equally deserving, heroes.

That he brought together such an impressive front line combination was perhaps his greatest feat. Had the side as a whole delivered the Holy Grail, he would have figured in the hall of greats. There are many who say that, had he strengthened the side in the year after promotion, the job would have been done. As it turned out, he handed the baton to an Irishman who was to bring a different approach.

9

Into the 1970s

Terry Neil came to Hull City from Arsenal in June 1970 as player-manager. The 28-year-old with 59 caps to his name had already skippered Northern Ireland with some distinction. Yet, for almost a year his promising career with the Gunners had been blighted by illness. Now fit again, his move to the Tigers had meant a substantial cut in wages. However, he was provided with an E-Type Jaguar and there were other incentives to take the Tigers to Division One. It was a new challenge.

George Best had once described Terry Neil as the worst manager he'd ever played for. However, Waggy has a different view based on his time at Hull City: 'Cliff was Cliff. He didn't have any favourites among the playing staff. Everybody was treated the same.

Dramatic goalmouth action: Hull City v. Blackpool, 23 January 1971. Hull City won 2-0 with goals from Chilton and Wagstaff. Chilton (third from left) scores with Waggy ever vigilant.

Terry Neil did things differently and, like many managers, it seemed that some players were his favourites. I got on very well with him and we became friends. Most of the players got on with him. In pre-season we used to do a little road work, running for a while then walking a bit before running again. As we built up, we'd do less walking until we could run all the way round. We'd go down Calvert Lane, through to the track behind the golf course down Wold Road, then through to Hessle and down Boothferry Road to the ground again.

'Under Terry we tended to do more running out at Brantingham and eventually our training was at the University. We tended to do more ball work than previously. For example, we'd practise chipping the goalkeeper from the edge of the box. Of course, we still did running and there was still an emphasis on creating space in terms of tactics. Weight training was introduced. Perhaps the game was a bit faster under Terry.' It was no secret though that the Irishman's ultimate aim was to manage Arsenal. In that sense, Hull was an expedient stepping-stone on the road to that ambition. Neil made his League debut against Swindon on 15 August 1970. He'd taken over a Hull side that had enjoyed a decade of reasonable success, but for whom promotion to Division One had remained elusive.

Drama at Boothferry Park: Hull City played Brentford in the fifth round of the FA Cup on 13 February 1971; the Tigers won 2-1. Ken Wagstaff (crouched) checks on the injured Chris Chilton. Also injured, Brentford's Bobby Ross.

FA Tour 1971 – raring to go.

The arrival of any new regime at a football club raises expectations and fuels hopes of success. Many felt that the long-awaited climb into Division One was largely a matter of tightening up defensively and providing a spark in midfield. Neil himself pulled on the number five shirt, at a stroke bringing on board composure, stability and leadership. His international class soon became evident. The opening League game of the season also saw a debut for Roger De Vries in the left-back position. It was to be the first of 350 appearances for the club. Roger was consistent and reliable at the back – a player with composure and ability. It was much needed at the time. Chris Simpkin continued in midfield that season. He was strong, dependable and a superb player, particularly in his forward runs. Billy Wilkinson was also still around. An excellent player, he'd played in several different roles. For most of the 1970/71 campaign he was in midfield.

On 1 August 1970, the Tigers met Peterborough United in the Watney Cup. Waggy and Chillo sank the Posh with two goals apiece. The victory brought a glamour tie against Manchester United and the opportunity for Waggy to play against his long-standing football hero – Denis Law.

Four days later, United came to Boothferry Park in the semi-final of the competition. The Watney Cup had been conceived as a means of bringing together high-scoring clubs from each of the divisions in the Football League. In all, eight teams participated – two from each of the divisions. Excluded were promotion sides or those who had qualified for European competition.

The Tigers had easily disposed of Peterborough United – scoring four goals in the spirit of the competition – and without reply. In the previous round, The Red Devils had nosed ahead in a five-goal thriller against Reading. They came to Boothferry Park expecting a win. Although the game was a pre-season affair, it was certainly not greeted with apathy by the 34,007 fans inside Boothferry Park. They witnessed one of the most thrilling encounters in the club's long history.

In fact, the game went down in football history as the first to be settled in a penalty shoot-out competition when the scores remained level after extra time. Hull's Ian McKechnie also earned his place in the record books by becoming the first 'keeper ever to save a penalty by that method of settling a game. The system had been adopted by FIFA and UEFA and was being used on an experimental basis.

The game began at a frenetic pace with both sides showing promise. The Tigers struck first in the 11th minute as Chris Chilton latched on to a failed clearance after Mally Lord had drifted a ball into the United area. His volley flew into the roof of the net with 'keeper Alex Stepney a stunned spectator.

The Tigers continued to press United for the rest of the half. The second 45 minutes began in similar fashion, but gradually United fought their way back. Twelve minutes from time, Best and Morgan combined well to set up Law for the equaliser. Extra time was played out with both sides struggling for the winner. Ian Mckechnie did well to smother a Best close-range attempt late on.

Two minutes from the end of what had become an epic struggle, Ken Wagstaff was brought down in the penalty area. It was an immensely dramatic moment in a highly charged atmosphere. The ground erupted in one voice crying for a penalty, but referee

Chris Chilton with typical aerial supremacy heads home in the Tigers' 5-2 victory over Leyton Orient at Boothferry Park, 17 April 1971. Goals went to Chilton (2), Wagstaff (2) and Ian Butler.

Finney waved play on. Waggy remembers the incident with remarkable clarity: 'As the final whistle blew, both sides found themselves in unknown territory. The tension in the ground was palpable. Could the Tigers dump the mighty Manchester United out of the competition and reach the final? A replay was not necessary. It had to be decided there and then.'

George Best, Brian Kidd and Bobby Charlton each notched up goals for United with Terry Neil, Ian Butler and Ken Houghton replying for Hull. With the score at 3-3, Hull City goalkeeper Ian McKechnie remembers seeing Denis Law lining up his sights.

'I knew Denis from my earlier career,' recalls Ian. 'His shot was low to my right. Some newspapers said Denis had missed. Not scoring is a miss but I had to dive at full stretch to save it!'

In that moment, all eyes in the ground were on Ken Wagstaff. Although he had a remarkable goalscoring record, his goals were scored mostly with his feet. In the early days at Mansfield, players had ribbed him about the lack of aerial strikes. In reply he chuckled, 'You play football with your feet. If God had wanted you to score with your head, he would have put boots there.'

That sense of humour was in fact not only a characteristic of Waggy's personality, but it was reflected in his often unpredictable, but always successful, style of play. Time after time, it paid dividends in normal play but penalties were something else. History records that Waggy missed the penalty. It fails to note that at least he'd had the courage to take it.

'I hated taking penalties,' he says. 'It was the same with headers. I only scored a few with my head. Denis Law was a great hero of mine. We spoke before he took his kick. It seemed it was a real pain for him having to think about the possibility of actually having to play in the final of what it seemed he felt was a bit of a Mickey-Mouse competition. He said he'd planned to play golf on the day of the final! I'm not sure how much that affected his miss! I went up to take the penalty and put Denis's golfing plans in jeopardy again! It made the scores even.'

At that point, the tie was still in the melting pot. The scores were simply levelled. What happened next was remarkable. Willie Morgan netted for United and it was City's turn to try and level the scores again. Instead of the next player stepping forward to take the kick, there seemed to be a debate going on in the middle of the field.

Goalkeeper Ian McKechnie was deep in conversation with his counterpart Alex Stepney. Neither expected to be

John Kaye, Hull City. The ex-West Brom midfielder shored up the Tigers' defence in the early 1970s and went on to manage the club.

Hull City *v.* Blackpool, FA Cup fourth round, 23 January 1971. Blackpool goalkeeper Taylor punches the ball clear with Wagstaff looking on.

called up at least until all the others had failed to settle matters. Yet, McKechnie found himself the subject of a plea from coach John McSeveney: 'I couldn't believe it. Ian Butler and I had got to the final of a penalty knock-out competition in the close season but to be asked to take a penalty on the spur of the moment was a big shock. Then, the referee came up and asked us to get on with it because he had a train to catch! My aim was to put the ball in the top right-hand corner of the goal. I took three paces back and hit it as hard as I could with my left foot. It cannoned off the post and ended up in the stand. I don't think Stepney got a touch, although some press reports say he saved it.'

Hull City: McKechnie, Beardsley, De Vries, Wilkinson, Neill, Simpkin, Lord, Houghton, Chilton (Pearson 87 min), Wagstaff, Butler.
Manchester Utd: Stepney, Edwards, Dunne (Stiles 115 min), Crerand, Ure, Sadler, Morgan, Law, Charlton, Kidd, Best.

With the new 1970/71 season approaching, the Tigers played a low-key friendly against Bradford City three days later. The match failed to attract more than 3,542 fans, but those that did turn up went home content with the 1-0 victory. The opening game of the season produced a 1-1 draw at Swindon. Certainly, the defence looked a little more solid.

It prompted a gate of almost 21,000 for the first home game of the season against Middlesbrough – a contest the Tigers won 1-0. Victory the following week at Watford brought Waggy's first League goal of the season. Not to be outdone, Chilton also netted in the 2-1 win. Carlisle upset the apple cart three days later, grabbing two goals without reply.

Aside from a 1-0 away defeat to West Ham United in the Football League Cup, the Tigers claimed three victories and a draw from their next four games. Scoring a total of eight goals, they'd kept three clean sheets – conceding only three during the draw at Bristol City.

The final game of that run against Norwich City at Carrow Road saw the dismissal of Chris Chilton for retaliation. It was a rare event, but one that had been provoked by a series of dubious challenges and tackles that had gone unpunished by the referee. To a great extent Chilton's speed had helped keep some distance from the boot boys. However, in the end, he'd had enough it seemed and in the eyes of the referee reacted inappropriately. Neil was taking a grip at the back while still trying to ensure that the front-runners had their chances. The Irishman had firmly in mind the goal of promotion.

For Waggy, the new boss offered some continuity with the promise of improvements to the side: 'Terry had pretty much the same ideas as Cliff really in as much as we had to find spaces, lose the markers and try to grab those chances that came up. It was tougher in Division Two. There were fewer chances and fewer sucker teams. It was about keeping it tight at the back, getting the ball forward and making sure we scored. The team was pretty well drilled and we still had the ability to challenge for promotion – particularly after the defence had been improved.'

Waggy has never suffered fools gladly, and it is testimony to Neil that the relationship with the City striker was based on mutual respect and not in small part by a sense of humour. Before one particular game, Ken recalls being handed a postcard by Neil. The handwritten card was addressed to:

'KEN WAGSTAFF (A DEADLY FINISHER IN THE BOX)'

On the reverse side were written the following instructions:

'GOAL SCORING FORWARD
BE ALERT FOR EVERYTHING IN BOX
(FLICK-ONS, MISTAKES ETC.)
FOLLOW IN SHOTS BY TEAM-MATES
PRESSURE DEFENDERS WHEN WE LOSE POSSESSION
MAKE THE JOB OF MARKING YOU DIFFICULT
(MOVE ABOUT)
SCORE USUAL GOALS
GOOD LUCK'
Terry

Just when the Tigers seemed to be on a roll, Birmingham City stepped in with a 1-0 victory. However, Neil was fielding a reasonably settled side and managed thereafter to

Boothferry Park drama in the Watney Cup, 5 August 1970. Hull goalkeeper Ian McKechnie saves with Manchester United's Brian Kidd challenging.

grab four successive victories – all clean sheets. Indeed, in the final game of that sequence against Charlton on 21 October, the Tigers had maintained eight clean sheets in 13 League games and averaged a superb rate of 0.62 goals conceded per game.

They had scored a total of 18 goals, taking the points from 9 wins, two draws and two defeats. Now things really were looking up and 25,340 fans turned up to watch the side earn a draw against Sheffield United on 24 October with a Waggy goal to send them home happy. At that point he was reasonably content with the way things were turning out: 'We did feel that the tide had turned. Mally Lord was putting in some good displays getting forward. Chillo was out there being Chillo, and we continued to do our thing successfully. There weren't that many chances coming up, but when they came, we put them away. Games were being won by small margins. We were tight at the back. It was a matter of grinding out results and it seemed to be working.'

It was therefore something of a shock to go to Cardiff City and take a five-goal battering! The result had the Tigers reeling, for they lost their next game 2-0 at home to Luton Town. Both Luton and Cardiff were useful sides that season finishing sixth and third in the table respectively. The setbacks were viewed in that light and there remained confidence that the Tigers could now move forward and at least challenge for promotion.

Oxford were no match for the Tigers. Chilton, Wagstaff and Houghton pressed home the point in a 3-0 lesson in how to win comfortably away from home. Queens Park Rangers and Portsmouth brought draws and matches against Leicester (3-0) and Blackburn (1-0) provided early-December optimism. However, Middlesbrough nudged a 1-0 victory on 19 December and spoiled the pre-Christmas festivities.

Although the Tigers had to share the points, a thrilling home game against Sheffield Wednesday on Boxing Day gave 24,399 fans a real treat, with goals for Chilton (2), Wagstaff and Houghton.

The 14 November game at Oxford had marked the start of a purple patch for Chris Chilton who notched up 11 League goals in the space of nine matches, including a hat-trick in the 4-0 defeat of Sunderland at Boothferry Park on 9 January. Waggy's strike in that game demonstrated his lightning reactions. Roger De Vries had a first-hand view: 'I did an overlap with Ian Butler and cut it back from the line to Chillo in the middle. He hammered it at the 'keeper who parried. The ball was travelling at great speed and it fell to Waggy. As ever, he was in exactly the right place. With virtually no reaction time he slammed it into the net. It was almost instantaneous.'

Charlton were the next scalp a week later by the only goal of the game. As ever, Waggy played his part in feeding the goal-ace with chances and netted three times himself in the same period his partner had run riot. He recalls: 'It certainly was a good run for Chillo. We got five wins and three draws in that spell. I remember the two home games against Sheffield Wednesday and then Sunderland when we scored four in each, with Chillo getting five. The draw against Wednesday was a real thriller.'

Division Two Table up to and including Saturday 23 January, 1971

	P	W	D	L	F	A	Pts
1 HULL CITY	25	14	6	5	39	24	34
2 Luton Town	24	12	8	4	38	17	32
3 Cardiff City	25	12	8	5	42	23	32
4 Leicester City	25	13	6	6	39	25	32
5 Sheffield Utd	25	11	9	5	43	30	31
6 Middlesbrough	25	12	6	7	37	29	30
7 Norwich City	25	9	11	5	31	26	29
8 Carlisle Utd	25	9	10	6	35	28	28
9 Swindon Town	25	10	7	8	36	25	27
10 Millwall	25	10	6	9	35	28	26

Although Portsmouth caused a surprise with their 1-0 win at Boothferry Park on 30 January 1971, for the rest of that season and but for the odd reversal, the Tigers kept

5 August 1970. Ian McKechnie dives to save a spot-kick from Manchester United's Denis Law. It was the first time a save had been made in the newly introduced penalty shoot-outs to decide tied games.

things extremely tight at the back, conceding only 16 goals in the same number of games. In the same period, they scored 15 times – registering seven draws, four defeats and five wins.

March saw the transfer of Alan Jarvis to Mansfield Town – Waggy's old club. He became the Stags' most expensive buy but unfortunately his career was eventually curtailed by serious injury. In the same month, Terry Neil paid a club-record fee of £60,000 for Ken Knighton. The Blackburn Rovers player was solid in the tackle and able to frustrate opposition attacks. Going forward, he was incisive and thoughtful.

Also joining the club at that time was Bill Baxter. He'd been a key player in Ipswich Town's League Championship season 1961/62 and it was hoped that his solid defensive track record coupled with an ability to score important goals would push the Tigers that one notch closer to the magic formula. Both players made their debuts in the Battle at Bramall Lane on 9 March 1971. It was a Yorkshire derby with a supercharged atmosphere with both clubs slugging it out for promotion.

Having been victorious at Sheffield on 9 March, the Tigers lost 1-0 at home to Oxford. If that wasn't enough of a setback, they followed it up with a 3-1 away defeat at Luton. With the vital points slipping away, City battled at Bolton Wanderers for a goal-less draw. Including that game, only four goals were scored by any side in the next 5 matches – resulting in 3 draws and 2 wins for the Tigers. It wasn't enough to pull off a promotion place.

The season ended in mixed fashion. A 5-2 home win against Orient on 17 April was followed by a 4-0 defeat at Millwall. The roller coaster ride continued its downward plunge with a 2-1 home defeat against Carlisle. The final match of the season ended in a 1-0 victory at Boothferry Park. The Tigers finished fifth in the Division Two table on 51 points, within reach of achieving what had for years seemed the impossible. They had been so near – yet so far.

In Ken's mind: 'Terry had changed things around and played a part himself in tightening up at the back.'

Final League Positions 1970/71

	P	W	D	L	F	A	W	D	L	F	A	Pts
1 Leicester City	42	12	7	2	30	14	11	6	4	27	16	59
2 Sheffield United	42	14	6	1	49	18	7	8	6	24	21	56
3 Cardiff City	42	12	7	2	39	16	8	6	7	25	25	53
4 Carlisle United	42	16	3	2	39	13	4	10	7	26	30	53
5 HULL CITY	42	11	5	5	31	16	8	8	5	23	25	51
6 Luton Town	42	12	7	2	40	18	6	6	9	22	25	49
7 Middlesbrough	42	13	6	2	37	16	4	8	9	23	27	48
8 Millwall	42	13	5	3	36	12	6	4	11	23	30	47
9 Birmingham City	42	12	7	2	30	12	5	5	11	28	36	46
10 Norwich City	42	11	8	2	34	20	4	6	11	20	32	44
11 QPR	42	11	5	5	39	22	5	6	10	19	31	43
12 Swindon Town	42	12	7	2	38	14	3	5	13	23	37	42

That season, Ken had missed only four games. In 38 appearances, he'd scored 12 goals, a measure perhaps of the reduced opportunities up front. One of the pleasant diversions earlier in the season had been a special game played at Craven Park to raise money for the National Youth Theatre Appeal and the Hull Arts Centre. A Tom Courtenay XI played the Youth Theatre Casuals. The game was refereed by City manager Terry Neil. Linesmen were none other than Chris Chilton and Ken Wagstaff.

Ken recalls: 'Tom was a really keen Hull City supporter among many others, including Barrie Rutter, Alan Plater and John Alderton to name but a few. Rodney Bewes was one of Tom's pals and we were proud to have them all among our supporters. Sometimes they'd be in the dug out and came into the dressing room. Charity games are a great

Penalty miss, 5 August 1970: McKechnie slams his spot-kick against the bar, becoming the first goalkeeper to miss a penalty in the newly introduced shoot-out phase.

way of raising money for worthy causes. In the game at Craven Park we had Rodney Bewes – who'd been at the Chelsea game at Stamford Bridge – Michael Parkinson, Marty Feldman, Alan Plater, Barrie Rutter, Kenny Lynch and several other showbusiness stars. Chris Chilton was linesman with me and I think he ran on the pitch and headed a goal. He obviously just couldn't resist it!'

The 1970/71 season had brought another good FA cup run. In the third round, the Tigers disposed of Charlton Athletic 3-0 at Boothferry Park through goals by Wagstaff, Houghton and Butler. The game on 2 January was played in front of almost 20,000 spectators. Although he'd scored himself, Ian Butler recalls an exceptional goal from Waggy: 'I recall having the ball out on the left wing and crossing it towards Chris Chilton in the middle. Chillo dummied the defender and let the ball through his legs to Waggy who instantaneously lashed it into the top right-hand side of the net from 30 yards out. It was so fast, the 'keeper never even saw it.

The strike once more demonstrated Waggy's speed of thought, immense power and clinical accuracy, not only at close range, but from outside the box.

In the next round, on 23 January 1971, they faced Blackpool at home in front of 34,752 hopeful supporters. Once again, Waggy and Chillo found the net in the Tigers' 2-0 win. Another Boothferry tie in the fifth round against Brentford drew in a gate of 29,709. Goals by Houghton and Chilton put City in the sixth round against Stoke City – yet again at home.

On 6 March 1971 the Tigers lined up against the Potters. Boothferry Park was packed with 41,452 supporters in the ground. Waggy loved the big occasions. From the whistle, the game flowed from end to end at a frenetic pace. It was a classic cup tie with neither side taking any prisoners in the tackle. In the seventh minute, Waggy lost the ball after a forceful Simpkin run. In typically determined fashion, he regained possession and pulled the ball back to Chilton who struck a powerful left-foot shot over the bar.

City's midfield were performing well in the tackle. Malcolm Lord's work rate was exemplary and Simpkin's forward runs were vital in supplying the ball to Chilton and Wagstaff, who were being tightly marked. Yet Smith in the Stoke defence often strayed too far up. In those lapses of concentration, the space was fully utilised by Lord and Wagstaff.

The Tigers' first goal came in the 14th minute from a move started by Terry Neil. The Irishman was excellent from set pieces. His free-kick to the edge of the penalty box was headed out but only as far as Chris Simpkin. Out of the tussle, the ball rolled free to Houghton who was unmarked midway through the Stoke half. His diagonal cross was perfectly flighted behind a goal-bound Butler with the defender committed to running with him. The winger checked his run, thereby creating the space and time to head first time across the box to Wagstaff lurking in the middle.

In the following seconds, Waggy further demonstrated the essence of his special magic. The high ball from Butler was effortlessly chested down past the advancing defender, who was sidestepped to the right with embarrassing ease. In a flash, with the crowd screaming for him to shoot, Waggy resisted and instead tapped clear of a second defender. A split second later, he foiled another tackle by shooting into the left-hand corner of the goal past a diving Gordon Banks.

Effectively, in the blink of an eye, he had beaten three defenders and a top-class international goalkeeper with cool, assured, poise that can only be described as awesome. In the space of those few seconds he demonstrated ball control, lightning speed and complete awareness that made top-quality players look like rank amateurs.

A short while later, Ian McKechnie's long powerful kick had sent Wagstaff on a run that finally ended in a free-kick. His deceptive pace and great power had allowed him to shrug off the defender, who by then had been exposed to the referee's wrath. In fact, Waggy had used a special tactic throughout his career to put the defenders at a disadvantage: 'On a run, if the defender could keep up at pace alongside, at the right moment I'd cut in slightly causing him to lose momentum. In that second, it was easier to pull away, often leaving no option but to rescue the situation with a foul.'

The move that led to Waggy's second goal started with a Malcolm Lord throw from midway in the Tigers' half on the right side of the field. The ball fell to Houghton just short of the halfway line. Houghton clipped it straight back. By now, Lord had spotted Wagstaff moving away from the goal on the edge of the box, with the defender behind him. His forward pass was perfectly flighted. Waggy moved towards the incoming ball.

Relaxing in Scarborough before the vital FA Cup quarter-final match at Boothferry Park on March 6 1971. From left to right: Chris Chilton, Billy Wilkinson and Ken Wagstaff.

In beating the defender to the header, he had sprung the trap. In the instant, the ball was laid off to Chilton, who was nearby in the centre. Waggy began a thundering goalwards run in anticipation of the inevitable return pass. That it came was a function of the brilliant understanding between the two players. Waggy had beaten the defender to it, rode a fierce tackle and left him for dead. It was part of the individual brilliance that had begun seconds before. One against one with Banks, Waggy had several options, the most obvious of which being to shoot powerfully towards goal. Instead, he kept his cool in a split second of deliberate hesitation. In that hiatus, the 'keeper

Hull City in the early 1970s. From left to right, back row: Geoff Barker, Malcolm Lord, Ian McKechnie, Chris Simpkin. Front row: Alan Jarvis, Tom Wilson, Don Beardsley, Frank Banks, Ken Wagstaff, Ian Butler, Terry Neil, Paddy Greenwood, Ray Pettit, Chris Chilton, Ken Houghton, Billy Wilkinson.

committed himself for the anticipated strike. Having forced Banks to play his only card, Waggy touched the ball to the right side of the 'keeper and into the net.

Former Hull and Mansfield player David Coates has a clear view on the goal: 'Most players in that situation would strike the ball against the 'keeper or across him but coolly Ken deceived Banks, who was desperate to smother the anticipated strike. With the 'keeper committed, he simply slid it past.'

Unfortunately, Stoke came back into the game as a result of several defensive lapses. In the end the Tigers lost the game 3-2. It was a bitter defeat for the fans, the players and the management of the club, all of whom had hoped for further progress in the competition.

Waggy's great hero Denis Law waxed lyrical about Ken's performance against Stoke. 'I must say, I felt sorry for Ken Wagstaff. To have put two goals past Gordon Banks and then see it all crumble away, he must have felt really sick. He's some player, brilliant in the box – as good as I've seen.'

125

Match programme for Republic of Ireland v. England: Ken Wagstaff plays at FA representative level in Dublin prior to a tour of Australasia.

FA tour of Australasia, 1971. Ken Wagstaff and Chris Chilton – centre left and right respectively talk with officials of an Australian club.

During the summer of 1971 Chris Chilton and Ken Wagstaff were selected for an FA representative side to tour Australasia. It was a just reward for the pair. There is little doubt that, had they played in Division One, full international honours would have followed. The team played in various locations and both players came home with enviable scoring records, having done themselves no harm for future selection. Ken recalls: 'We had some really funny training sessions out there in Australia. They wanted Chillo and I to do the same double act as we were doing at Hull. The problem was that every time Chillo went up to head a ball, this other England player used to charge up and try and head it at the same time. In the end, I went up to the manager and told him the twat was getting in Chillo's way. In fact it was Dave Watson, who ended up playing centre half in the end!'

10

Kaye's Era: Kaye Sera

There was a distinctly Continental flavour about the build up to the 1971/72 season. Thanks to Terry Neil, the Tigers found themselves in Scandinavia. This is where Waggy and Chillo were required to fly on their return from the England tour, for the Tigers' pre-season build-up.

Chris Chilton did not join the party in Sweden and Waggy missed the winning games against, Sandviken IF and AIK Stockholm. However, he joined the team for the final against Halmstad, who were one of Sweden's top sides. In a convincing 6-1 win to take the Stockholm July Cup, Waggy scored a hat-trick. It was a far cry from the English Division Two, but excellent pre-season preparation nonetheless.

Ken recalls: 'I remember Terry organizing some sort of outward bound training for us in a massive forest. It should have been a four-hour hike following blue or red routes for two separate parties. In theory, it was more of a walking exercise than map reading. One party were still out there completely lost after eight hours and had to be rescued!'

Certainly, the experience didn't affect the Tigers' ability to find the goal. On 4 August they hammered a Japan XI 5-0. Certainly, on that day, it was the opposition that had lost their way!

The line-up for the first League game of the season still boasted the talented forwards that had been tried and tested in battle. With an excellent first term under his belt and with several new signings to ice the cake, it was an optimistic Terry Neil that ran out to face Charlton on 14 August 1971. City lost 1-0.

A week later at Boothferry Park, the 1-0 victory against Oxford United was momentous only in that it was the last-ever League game played by the great Chris Chilton for Hull City. It was the end of a sensational strike partnership that had thrilled spectators all over the country. In many ways it was a sad day for both players: 'Chris was a special player and a special person,' says Ken. 'We had an extremely successful partnership on the field and off the field we were the best of friends. There was a mutual respect and a great understanding. I was very sad to see him go but I think he wanted Division One football sooner rather than later. As time went by, it became ever more difficult for both of us. Hull were ambitious and we'd hoped to be in the top League with them.'

The arrival of Tommy Docherty at Hull City as Terry Neil's assistant was not greeted with a champagne toast in all parts of the dressing room. Indeed, some former players have since expressed grave dissatisfaction with the Doc's influence. All the evidence emerging suggests that Chris Chilton did not see eye to eye with the Scot and had little or no respect for him. On top of that, the City star had not exactly seen eye to eye with Neil, at least over the issue of a close-season trip abroad that had followed the FA tour of Australasia.

At the time, the *Hull Daily Mail* reported in an interview with Chris Chilton that the player had wanted Division One football with Hull City. In the feature, Chilton acknowledged the wonderful understanding with Ken Wagstaff and confirmed the instinctive nature of their interplay on the field.

Without doubt, Chilton was one of the all-time Hull City greats. With 218 goals to his credit in 477 League and cup games, he remains the holder of the club's all-time top-scoring record. He was a positive influence both in the dressing room and on the field. He and Waggy were close friends yet individuals – some say like chalk and cheese. On the field their partnership was 22-carat gold. And now it was over.

Chilton's replacement was Stuart Pearson. He never approached the scoring feats of his predecessor but he was a new talent all the same and someone who would grace hallowed arenas elsewhere in due course. Pearson wore the number 9 jersey 38 times that season scoring 15 League goals.

'Stuart was very fast off the mark,' says Ken. 'He made quite a lot of goals. He could shoot quickly and although he didn't break any records at Hull, it was clear that he had a natural gift for scoring.'

The Oxford victory marked a spell of three wins and a draw including a notable 1-0 victory against Birmingham City at Boothferry Park in front of 16,746 spectators. In four of the first five games of the season, the points had been decided by a single goal in

Long-serving Jimmy Lodge chats with manager Terry Neil and Les Moody – one of the newest members of the club's staff.

Waggy in a goalmouth duel. Hull City *v.* Birmingham's Division Two clash on 1 September 1971. The Tigers won 1-0.

each game. However, hopes that the show was finally on the road were dashed by a 4-0 away defeat to Bristol City. Portsmouth and Carlisle continued the gloomy losing trend in successive games.

Roy Greenwood, who had signed apprentice forms in August 1968, was blooded into the first team on 29 September against Swindon Town. Although the game ended in a 2-0 victory for the Tigers, a draw and two defeats followed. Questions were again being asked of the City defence and the answers were not long in arriving.

Waggy had played in the first eight League games of the season, scoring only on his last outing in the 2-1 away defeat at Carlisle on 25 September. In the next 10 League games, he missed five through injury. His only goal in that spell came in the victory against Watford on 20 October. After that game, the Tigers suffered five successive defeats. Only a goal-less draw against Millwall on 27 November had prevented that being extended to seven matches as the Tigers then lost to Sheffield Wednesday on 4 December.

Goals were hard to come by and in the first 20 games of the season, City had lost 12, drawn 3 and won only 5 games. August optimism had been replaced with the chill December winds of reality. It was not to be the final push to Utopia. Instead, it was a slow grind to mid-table mediocrity once more.

October saw the introduction of Jimmy McGill to the midfield. His transfer from Huddersfield brought a linkage with the playmakers Houghton and Knighton, and the indefatigable Malcolm Lord.

McGill was a real character and stories abound about the player's humour. In one game, the manager had left him out of the side. Having gone to Neil's hotel room to protest, he received no response. Frustrated and angry, it is alleged that he then acquired a plank that had been left lying about the corridor. Only the sudden and chance intervention by a hotel employee prevented him from using it as a battering ram to gain entry to Neil's room!

In an attempt to beef up the side's defence further, Neil also brought John Kaye to the club from West Bromwich Albion in November 1971. His acquisition added a good deal of steel, drive and experience to the side. Goole-born Kaye started his career with Scunthorpe United in September 1960, playing as a forward. His move to West Bromwich Albion in May 1963 saw him adopt a midfield role. He won an FA Cup winners' medal in 1968, a Football League Cup winners' medal in 1966 and Football League Cup final runners-up medals in 1967 and 1970. In 284 games for West Brom, he scored 45 goals.

On 11 December, Middlesbrough came to Boothferry Park. The clash sparked a seven-goal encounter with the points going to City thanks to goals by John Kaye (2), Stuart Pearson and Frank Banks. It wasn't until 22 January that Waggy ended a League drought of 12 games without scoring. The Tigers lost 2-1 to Swindon at Boothferry Park. However, that game marked the start of a six-game spell during which he would score seven goals. Watford were then thrashed 4-0 at Boothferry Park before Burnley fell 2-0. Both games featured Waggy goals.

Preston North End provided the next thrilling all-action encounter for a Boothferry crowd of more than 14,000. Now on song, it took just three minutes for Wagstaff to

A postcard from abroad. With Waggy recovering from injury, his team-mates send a glossy postcard from a training camp in Sweden 1972.

open the scoring. In a period of intense opening pressure that had involved two corners and a free-kick from Terry Neil, the ball finally fell to Waggy, who converted the chance with a rapid strike just inside the post. In the 28th minute, another free-kick from Neil sparked a right-wing interplay with Lord and Banks. Finally the ball was crossed to Pearson whose strike was blocked. The rebound fell to Wagstaff who thrashed it into the net without ceremony. The game ended 3-2 to the Tigers.

After a 1-1 draw against Orient, City went on to register a notable 4-0 home victory against Fulham on 11 March. Waggy was made man of the match and the headline 'WIZARD WAGSTAFF' was one of a clutch of superlatives used to describe his performance. Not only had he scored two goals himself, but his play had also created a pair for partner Stuart Pearson. In both cases, he had provided telling and perfectly weighted passes. Not even the on-loan Alan Mullery in the Fulham defence could repress the still-potent City forward line. Waggy recalls: 'It was Jeff Wealand's debut. He was deputising for the injured McKechnie and made three fantastic point-blank saves. Billy Wilkinson and Jimmy McGill played brilliantly in midfield.'

Waggy scored at Bristol City on 25 March and his opportunist goal at Sunderland on April Fools' Day broke a deadlock in appalling weather conditions. Due to an injury sustained against Luton Town, Waggy took no further part in the season's fixtures and the side ended up in 12th place.

Despite the disappointing League campaign, City did progress to the fifth round of the FA Cup. Having disposed of Norwich in the third round, fate dealt an interesting tie

Ian Gaunt presents the North Midlands League Cup to Ken Wagstaff in April 1974. The Tigers reserves won the trophy with two Wagstaff goals on his way back from injury.

Hull City squad, 1973/74. From left to right, back row: Terry Neil, Frank Banks, Ken Knighton, Don Beardsley, Ian McKechnie, Jeff Wealands, Stuart Blampey, Roger De Vries, Paul O'Riley. Front row: John Kaye, Jimmy McGill, Stuart Pearson, Phil Holme, Ken Wagstaff, Malcolm Lord, Ron Greenwood, Stephen Deere.

at Coventry City – Chris Chilton's new club! England boss Alf Ramsey was in the crowd. He'd regularly passed over both Wagstaff and Chilton in selections for full international honours.

Chilton led the Coventry side out to great applause from the Hull contingent in a crowd of almost 25,000 fans. However, once the game had kicked off, it was Coventry's supporters initially that took up the roar, albeit for only a matter of seconds. They were suddenly shocked into silence as Waggy almost scored inside the first minute. From a free-kick, Terry Neil had found him lurking unmarked inside the penalty area. His low shot was parried by a diving Bill Glazier and the ball was hooked clear in desperation as Pearson and Lord closed in for the kill.

On 15 minutes, Hull 'keeper Ian McKechnie finger-tipped over the bar a 25-yard scorcher from Quentin Young. From a half-cleared corner, Jimmy McGill shot from the edge of the box and almost settled the stalemate with a powerful drive. It was a typically full-blooded cup tie and the game needed a match winner. It came in the 76th minute as Waggy demonstrated the opportunist dimension to his play. A strike on goal from the tireless Frank Banks had rebounded off the post. Ever in the right place

John Kaye leads out Hull City for the final of the Watney Cup at Stoke on 18 August 1973. The Tigers lost 2-0.

at the right time, Waggy latched on to the rebound and rammed it home without undue drama.

After the match, Waggy received a flower from Hilary Needler, wife of the Hull City chairman: 'The sky-blue carnation had been given to Hilary Needler by Derrick Robins. Like any true City supporter, she decided not to wear the flower during the match. Afterwards, she presented it to me for scoring the winner. I still have that flower in a scrapbook as a reminder of the game.'

Having already fought a dramatic battle with Stoke the previous year in the sixth round, it was almost as if fate had intervened to bring the Tigers an early opportunity to settle the scores. Unfortunately, although Waggy managed to score, it was a lone effort in a disappointing 4-1 defeat. Earlier in the season, Liverpool had dumped the Tigers out of the Football League Cup in a 3-0 encounter at Anfield in front of 31,612. It had been another barren year in terms of honours, but one that left fans with plenty to talk about in years to come.

In the close-season Ken underwent two cartilage operations and missed the first seven League games. The 1972/73 season that followed was memorable, if only that it

A rare sight: Ken Wagstaff pictured in the dugout – sidelined due to injury. Coach John McSeveney (right) keeps his eye on the game.

marked a barren season of goals for Ken Wagstaff. It was hardly surprising, given that he only played in 16 League games due to recurrent problems including muscle and tendon strains. It was also another mediocre year with the Tigers again mid-table, this time securing 13th place.

However, another good run in the FA Cup had taken the side to the fifth round once more, with Waggy scoring in the third round replay against Stockport County. He missed the fourth round victory against West Ham United and also the defeat at Coventry City in the next round. It was a dismal and miserable season and a far-flung cry from the heady days in promotion year and the subsequent season when the side had headed Division Two for a while.

Winger Ian Butler left the Tigers for York City in July 1973 having fallen out of favour with Terry Neil, the man who he claims had once described him as the best left-footed forward in the game. Despite having scored in three consecutive games in November 1972, Butler had a difference of opinion with the manager on a disciplinary issue. Subsequently, there was talk of legal action as a result of press statements made by Neil, but the issue died away as Butler went on to help York to promotion in his first season.

Pre-season in 1973/74 brought an inspired Watney Cup run for the Tigers after defeating Mansfield Town and Bristol Rovers. Although there were hopes that there would be a more interesting trophy cabinet at Boothferry Park, the Tigers went down 2-0 to Stoke City in the final on 2 September.

In that League season, Waggy played in 32 League matches, netting eight times. Although the side improved its League position on the previous year finishing up in ninth place, they lacked the overall power to mount a serious challenge on the leaders. They had conceded 12 fewer goals, but had also scored 18 less than in the previous season.

The season marked the end of John Kaye's playing career with the club – his last game being the away Boxing Day clash at Sheffield Wednesday. However, he was retained on the coaching staff.

May 1974 had also seen the departure of Stuart Pearson for Manchester United. It was a remarkable success story for the local lad who went on to win FA and Football League Cup winners' medals, as well as England caps. His move would mark a crisis in the Tigers' attack as the team looked to recapture the magic formula that had endured previously with Chilton and Wagstaff.

Although FA Cup hopes had disappeared with a third-round exit to Bristol City, the Football League Cup had provided some highlights to the year. On 8 October a second-round tie at Leicester City with goals from Wagstaff, Galvin and a Whitworth own goal. In the replay at Boothferry Park, the Tigers emerged 3-2 victors. In the next round they faced Stockport County at home. City won with goals from Wagstaff, Holme and Banks.

In a keenly fought tie on 27 November 1973, the Tigers entertained Liverpool at Boothferry Park in front of almost 20,000 fans. The goal-less draw brought a replay at Anfield, which the Tigers lost 3-1.

The 1974/75 season started with some promise. Waggy scored in each of the three opening League games as draws against Southampton and Aston Villa were followed by a 1-0 defeat of West Bromwich Albion at Boothferry Park. However, in the next four matches, the Tigers would concede 12 goals without scoring and crash to three defeats without a single victory.

September brought a dramatic change in the club's leadership. Terry Neil was offered and accepted the job as manager of Tottenham Hotspur. In the next two years, he went on to improve the club's results. Then, in summer 1986 he took over from Bertie Mee as manager of Arsenal – his ambition achieved at last.

Meanwhile, at Boothferry Park a departing Neil had advised chairman Harold Needler to appoint John Kaye as manager. The advice was heeded and Kaye took over the reins. Essentially, he succeeded in developing a stronger defence, but some argued his sides lacked punch in forward positions, despite the continuing presence of Wagstaff. Looking back, Kaye reflected on the position: 'I tried to buy Alf Wood at the outset to partner Waggy. It was felt he could do a similar job to Chris Chilton. We landed him in the end, but he wasn't available as early as we would have liked. In the event, it didn't quite work out.' Still an effective striker, Waggy's speed was starting to wane a little. Although he could still beat players, getting away from them was less easy. The answer, was simplicity itself: 'By the 1974/75 season, I was starting to be troubled with injuries. Also, it wasn't so easy to beat defenders for pace. However, I could still go past them most of the time. The way round the problem was simply to get rid of the ball as soon as I'd gone past the man!'

Joining the Tigers in Division Two in 1974/75 was a Manchester United side determined to go back up in their first season following the ignominious drop. There seemed to be an air of inevitability about the rise. Although United took the championship, their trip to Boothferry Park on 23 November provided a shock result for the otherwise rampant Red Devils.

In a 2-0 victory to the Tigers before 23,287 fans, it was that man Wagstaff, together with Malcolm Lord, that saw off United. It was certainly a feather in the side's cap and demonstrated that they were far from a spent force. The United game marked the debut of Alf Wood, formerly of Millwall, Shrewsbury and Manchester City. Converted to a centre forward at Shrewsbury his scoring record was impressive, with a total of 40 in one season alone.

Up until the end of December, in the 25 League games played, the Tigers had won 8, drawn 9 and lost 8 games. They were at least holding their own. Having missed two matches in that period and due to injury, Ken played no part in the programme after the New Year. Despite the long lay off, he still ended up as the club's top goalscorer in that season with 10 goals to his credit.

It had not been a bad season for the Tigers who finished in eighth place in the table. They had not progressed beyond the third round of the FA Cup that season but it had taken two replays before Fulham prevailed in a 1-0 victory on neutral ground. Waggy had played only in the first match but managed to score. In a short spell in the reserves on his way back from injury Ken helped secure the North Midlands League Cup, scoring twice in the final.

In his last season at Boothferry Park, Ken scored twice in 10 League appearances. He'd also netted twice in the Anglo-Scottish Cup – once against his old club Mansfield. Waggy played his last game in the amber and black against Portsmouth on 22 November 1975 at Boothferry Park. It was another landmark in the history of a club that had seen many truly great players wear its colours. To a list that included Carter, Jenson, Mannion, Bly, Franklin, Mortenson, Revie and Chilton was now added the name Wagstaff.

In 1975 Ken was granted a benefit match. Many of his friends in the game and beyond contributed to the Testimonial Brochure. Actor Tom Courtenay recalled how he'd met Ken at the charity soccer match at Craven Park. After the game they became friends and eventually Tom gave the name 'Wagstaff' to his dalmatian. Once news of this leaked out, there was much hilarity in the dressing room. Players debated who was better

Match Programme. Hull City *v.* Liverpool Football League Cup fourth round 27 November 1973.

Ken Wagstaff, 1975.

Actor Tom Courtenay with his dog, Wagstaff.

looking – Waggy or the dog. In a classic quip, goalkeeper Ian McKechnie said: 'The dog's better looking, but Waggy's got more spots!'

Given that Sir Tom was a brilliant performer on film and television, he paid great compliment to Ken's acting skills by citing one of the player's little foibles in winning penalties and free kicks. He said: 'The game is full of great divers and fallers, but nobody can be poleaxed by a tackle, get the free-kick and be up and running with quite the drama and finesse of Waggy.' Tom referred to the 'fall' that he had once seen, after which his father said: 'He's a better actor than you!'

Tom's long-standing support for the club was repaid when the team turned up to be part of the surprise party when the actor was featured with Eamon Andrews on the TV programme *This Is Your Life*.

Ken Wagstaff's testimonial brochure 1975. Drawing by Alan Plater.

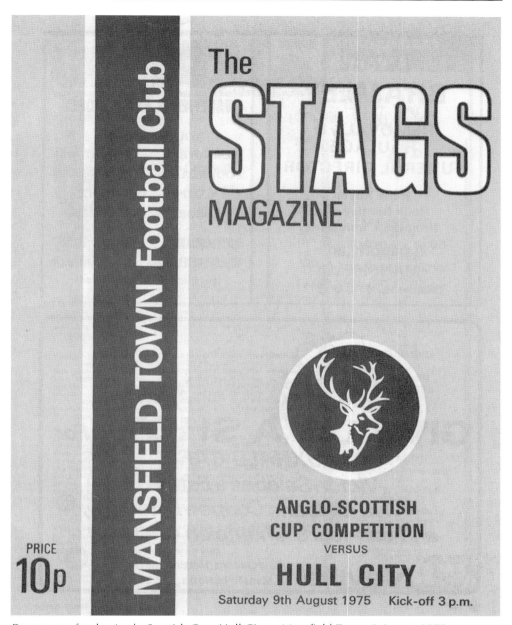

The STAGS MAGAZINE

MANSFIELD TOWN Football Club

PRICE 10p

ANGLO-SCOTTISH CUP COMPETITION
VERSUS
HULL CITY
Saturday 9th August 1975 Kick-off 3 p.m.

Programme for the Anglo-Scottish Cup. Hull City v. Mansfield Town, 9 August 1975.

The late Harold Needler was chairman of the club at the time of the testimonial. In his contribution to the brochure, he paid tribute to Ken's contribution to Hull City. He cited the unique mixture of joy, frustration, agony, ecstasy, hope and disappointment that he had felt during his years at the club. The chance to thank Waggy was a moment of '100 per cent pleasure.'

143

Hull City manager John Kaye plots tactics, January 1975.

Ken Wagstaff and his benefit committee.

Ken had the greatest respect for Mr Needler. He recalls how Harold, in his final days before succumbing to serious illness, had entered the dressing room to say goodbye to the players of his beloved club. In turn, he shook their hands. Finally, he sat next to Ken without speaking. As he rose, he tapped Ken's knee saying, 'Thanks.'

'Harold Needler was a great man and a great chairman for the club,' remembers Ken. 'In those days, players were not paid millions like some are today. He was a gentleman and someone who did what he could to help me in a personal sense.'

In a comprehensive career resume Brian Taylor of the *Hull Daily Mail* wrote about the highlights of Ken's career. In the final paragraph of the piece, he found prophetic words that have endured: 'Players like Ken Wagstaff come once in a lifetime if you are lucky, but nothing is more certain than the fact that, even on Humberside, it will be more than a lifetime before his name, his skill and his goals are forgotten.'

11

Now and Then

In the final days of his career at Boothferry Park, when he was troubled with injuries, Ken was called into John Kaye's office. The consultant had found damage to his cruciate ligament. In those days, it was regarded as a serious injury. Ken found himself running around doing little more than errands. He decided to go to Australia to be player-manager of George Cross – a Maltese team. The possibility had been discussed in a pub one day in Hull. He decided to give it a try: 'It was a wonderful opportunity to go out there and try my hand at management. They weren't a bad team and just needed some organisation. I played some games myself and found my knee getting stronger and stronger. The team did exceptionally well and won the league they were in, and a cup competition.'

After a while, Ken had to come home to sort out some personal matters. It was ex-Tiger and close friend Billy Wilkinson that took over Ken's management duties for a temporary period. For a while, it seemed that Ken's clean bill of health would allow a return to the Hull City first team. In fact, it seems the Football League blocked the move with the club having already claimed on a special insurance to cover what had been thought to be a career-ending injury. It was a disappointment. Ken tried unsuccessfully to reverse the decision: 'Later, I spoke personally to the consultant. He revealed that he'd advised the club that rest may help strengthen the knee and it could be right again. Instead, they had taken the insurance. Obviously, they had to make a judgement about risk and benefit. In Australia, the knee was fine. When I came back there was talk of a return at Hull City, but it wasn't possible because the insurance had been cashed. Had it not been for that, I might have been able to continue for another two or three years.'

Looking back, Ken recalls a personal gesture from the club chairman who had arranged a gratuity payment at the end of his service: 'Mr Needler paid some money into an account that still yields a small sum each month. I'm not sure how it was linked to the insurance payment received by the club, but it was certainly a kind gesture on his part.'

Ken enjoyed his time at both Hull City and Mansfield Town. Most of his career was spent with the Tigers and he recalls the wonderful spirit at the club: 'It was a great time. We all got on very well and used to go out together. We'd go to different pubs, have a drink and then later on in the evening meet up with wives and girlfriends for a meal.'

Behind the scenes, Waggy remembers the late club masseur Jimmy Lodge. A stout, dark-haired man, he'd been at the club for 50 years as player, trainer and masseur: 'Jimmy was a real character. He smoked like a chimney and had very rough hands. We used to dread having to have a massage. It was like being rubbed with sandpaper. Just before we had a massage, he'd say: "I'll put some olive oil on." He'd then take a swig from the bottle before pouring it on to his hands. Then he'd run it through his hair before using it as a massage oil!'

Ken also recalls some funny incidents with groundstaff: 'We had some fun with Stan Coombes the groundsman. The pitch was his pride and joy and we had to tread carefully. The lads pulled a few stunts, including one unspeakable incident by Keckers. However, Stan got his own back one day. He asked if he could take a penalty against McKechnie. There he was, in all his groundsman gear, including a big pair of wellies. He ran up and connected with the ball. It went wide. However, his boot flew off and hit Keckers right on the head!'

Looking back at the managers he worked with at Hull, Ken had great admiration for all three – Cliff Britton, Terry Neil and John Kaye: 'Cliff delivered promotion from Division Three and but for a failure to strengthen the defence, he could have taken us to the First. Terry Neil was an excellent footballer and had strengths as a manager, but his great ambition was to manage Arsenal. We came close to promotion to Division One with Terry. John Kaye did reasonably well. He was a great player and when he finished as manager, the team were mid-table in Division Two. That wasn't good enough for a small section of supporters. It's often those cynics that whip up unrest and cause directors to change direction when what may be needed is stability and patience.'

Having been divorced, Ken married Eileen in 1978 at Sutton Methodist Hall. Their daughter Francesca was born a year later.

Although Billy Wilkinson returned to England for holidays, he made his home in Australia. His life sadly ended there as a result of a heart attack aged just fifty-three. In accordance with his wishes, his ashes were scattered over the turf at Boothferry Park.

Hull City ex-players' reunion. From left to right: Ken Wagstaff, John McSeveney and David Coates.

Ken Wagstaff pictured as manager of the Plimsoll Ship Inn, Hull in 1982, hours before the FA Cup tie against Chelsea and sixteen years after his double strike at Stamford Bridge in the same competition.

1990s reunion: Former Hull City players Ken Wagstaff, Chris Chilton, Ken Houghton and John McSeveney pictured at a reunion dinner.

In the years since his retirement from football, Ken turned his hand to pub and club management – initially at the Plimsoll Ship Inn in Hull. Later, he became proprietor of the Marlborough Club at Hessle. In autumn 2002 he has taken on additional responsibilities in a new pub venture close to the new multi-million pound super stadium – the new home of Hull City Football Club. Ken lives happily in Hull with his wife Eileen and daughter Francesca. He keeps in touch with former team-mates in Hull and Mansfield through regular reunions and other events, including football matches with the ex-Tigers. In the early 1990s he collaborated with Chris Chilton in the making of a video entitled *Chillo and Waggy*. He has also periodically written articles in the local press.

Up until Raich's death, Ken had kept in touch with his former manager, friend and mentor who lived in Willerby, a village on the western outskirts of Hull: 'Raich and I always remained close and we would meet up at sports dinners and other events. He had a wealth of knowledge about the game and a host of stories and memories.'

Looking back on a brilliant career, Ken Wagstaff can take great pride in his achievements. Although he never played in Division One his reputation is carved indelibly in the history of English football. He always speaks highly of his strike partner Chris Chilton. Recently, at Waggy's sixtieth birthday party, the pair emerged to the acclaim of almost 300 guests at the Ramada Jarvis Hotel in Willerby.

In his club at Hessle, a village on western outskirts of Hull, Waggy often reminisces with friends in the bar. Often they tease him with remarks like: 'You didn't do a lot of

Ken Wagstaff, pursuing his golfing interests.

1990s – Waggy as occasional columnist for the *Hull Daily Mail*.

Wilf Pointon (father of Neil, the footballer), with his wife Marlene (Ken's sister) and a smiling Waggy.

running about.' The fact is, few players caught Waggy once he was clear. In the latter months of his career when he was slowing down, he used his football brain to overcome the problem: 'It was simple really. As I got older and perhaps lost a little pace, I'd still beat the forwards on the dribble and then pass the ball rather than trying to outstrip them on the run.'

On the terraces, Waggy and his partner Chris Chilton were regarded as greats in the club's history. Time has not faded that view. In a centenary poll conducted by the Football League, fans voted Waggy as the most popular Tiger of all time – eclipsing even the great Raich Carter. In the Hull City poll, he received a massive 54.1 per cent of the votes. Raich Carter was second – his support to some extent affected by the passage of time since his days at Boothferry Park. In third place was goalkeeper Billy Bly. Chris Chilton, Viggo Jenson and Andy Davidson each had 4.2 per cent of the vote.

Davidson and Chilton held records for highest club goalscorer and most appearances respectively. Jenson was a Danish international who had signed for City in 1948. A one-time forward, he was well-respected and played in several positions over the course of his career. Hull City Football Club, in the middle of moving to a new stadium, plan a

Ken Wagstaff pictured with skipper Andy Davidson as they take the field for a charity cricket match with the Lords Taverners.

Ex-Tigers take the field once more. Pictured during an occasional ex-Tigers match are, from left to right, Ken Wagstaff, Chris Chilton and Ian Butler.

series of end-of-era events, including honouring former players in various ways. Ken is very proud of the award: 'It was a great moment when I was told. The greatest honour was to be even considered in a poll that contained the great Raich Carter. I think the result was obviously affected by the fact that some of the players were from the club's past and the voters will never have seen the others play. In terms of the spirit of the award, then the affection of the people means more to me than any money and it is wonderful to be still recognised after the years have passed even since I played. The same comments apply for both Hull City and Mansfield and the recognition at both clubs is wonderful.'

That he received the same award for his previous club Mansfield Town speaks volumes about the man and his talent. Forty years after he graced the ground, he received a rapturous welcome at a packed Field Mill when the award was made by Joe Eaton on behalf of the club.

Ken openly acknowledged that the press often seemed to fasten on to the goalscorers and make them out to be the heroes, but this wasn't anything he could control. He knew that football is a team game and that each player deserves due credit for their part.

Match reports in local papers usually contained a balanced account. However, national papers usually had much shorter coverage and some tended to sensationalise events, building up the hype – and then often going out of their way to destroy their prey.

'I loved every minute of my time at Hull City,' says Ken. 'They were great days. Chris Chilton and I have talked since about our best moments. We agreed that one of the outstanding features of home matches was when we were on the attack. There was a wave of expectation in the crowd. Those at the front would stand, so those behind had to get up to see over them. Even when we went behind, they still cheered us because they expected us to score. It was like being at Wembley every home game!'

Looking back on the referees in his era, Waggy recognises that it wasn't an easy job. Sometimes, poor decisions would turn games – the Chelsea cup tie being a prime example. When aggrieved, he would speak to the referee, sometimes in passing. On occasion, he would appeal more directly, often with little success: 'They just used to

Winning smiles – Ken and his daughter Francesca in 1979.

Ken Wagstaff pictured in 1994 as proprietor of the Marlborough Club, Hessle, near Hull.

Ken and his daughter Francesca at the seaside in 1981.

ignore me. Players often gave them stick but they expected it. They just got on with the game. I think they should do more of that these days.'

A sense of humour is not unusual among players. However, referees are not commonly appreciated for their sense of humour. Waggy recalls top referee Gordon Hill's bizarre sense of fun. Having been stamped upon by an opposition player, Waggy had gone off at the referee's suggestion. Hill had said, 'Go off and get it seen to and just come on when you are ready.'

Of course, the helpful invitation was not in keeping with the norm. Players need to obtain the referee's sanction at the point of re-entry to the field of play. However, Waggy took the official literally and ran on as soon as he'd recovered. To his amazement Hill booked him! However, as the two walked off at the final whistle, Waggy learned that the referee was just winding him up!

One of Ken's long-standing pastimes is golf. It was an interest that he followed in his days at Hull City. Malcolm Lord recalls a game played in the late 1960s: 'Waggy and Chillo were playing golf one Thursday afternoon. In fact they shouldn't have been there at the time. Unfortunately, Waggy sliced the ball. Chillo was standing nearby and it hit him on the back of his calf. It swelled up to twice its normal size and he missed the next game! I also remember Ken borrowing my driver. We are both left-handed. When he brought it back it was in three pieces! He kindly said he'd replace it, but so far it has slipped his memory! Putting a memo in his book might help though!

Francesca, Ken and Eileen Wagstaff pictured relaxing at home in August 2002.

'Certainly, Ken had a particular brand of humour. The chairman Harold Needler always liked to hear Waggy say something before a game. One day just before kick-off at Blackpool he said: "We're going to get something from this game today, Chairman." Mr Needler's eyes lit up and he smiled. Quick as a flash Waggy followed up with: "We're gonna get a bloody good hiding." In fact, we were well beaten. Only Waggy could have got away with that.'

Until 1995, Waggy also played football occasionally with a local veterans' team. Organiser Eric Grubb, who informally scouted for the Tigers under Bob Brocklebank and Cliff Britton recalls: 'We used to play in various places, often down south. I hated losing to southern teams and put Ken on a £10-a-goal commission. Even in his 50s he would regularly pick up £100 over a weekend! One week, our centre half was badly injured and we were struggling to make up the numbers. We decided to play him out on the wing so that at least we could put 11 out. In reality he was crippled. Just before kick off one of their players asked: "Which one is Wagstaff?" Word had got around about his abilities and they wanted to target him. We told them it was the bloke out on the wing. They had two men on him throughout the game. The real Waggy scored four. As we left the pitch they pointed to him and said: "Who's that?"'

Ken and Eileen Wagstaff on their wedding day.

12

Talking about Waggy

Alan Plater

'It's a sure sign that you've known somebody a long time when you can't remember when you first met. That being so, most of what follows is guesswork. I can remember the first time I saw Ken. It was at Boothferry Park when he was playing for Mansfield and already making a name for himself by scoring 40 goals a season. My first impression was that he'd obviously learned something from his then manager, Raich Carter. He was strong on the ball, a deadly finisher, a shrewd reader of the game and highly skilled at persuading defenders to foul him in and around the penalty area.

'Then he signed for City and the rest is history, which you'll find elsewhere in this book. We all have our memorable Wagstaff goals, like the couple he stroked past Gordon Banks in the Stoke City cup tie in 1971. But one of my favourites in, I think, the same season was in an away match against Queens Park Rangers. Ken got the ball on the edge of the six-yard box, surrounded by defenders and then he did something – I don't know what it was – but they all seemed to run away from him! Then he rolled the ball gently into the net.

'Though he could wallop the ball with the best, many of his best goals were gentle trickles and lobs. He once said to me: 'All the ball has to do is cross the line.' All the great finishers, players like Greaves, Dalglish and Best, scored goals of that kind, and Ken belonged in that category. Though I'm delighted he stayed with City, it's tantalizing to think what might have happened if he'd moved to the top division in mid-career.

'I think the first time we met was probably when Terry Neil's first-team squad appeared on Tom Courtenay's *This Is Your Life*. I have to confess much of this is a blur because Ian McKechnie and I were the last to leave the bar after the show – anxious, I imagine, to maintain the reputations of goalkeepers and playwrights respectively.

'Subsequently I was a member of Ken's testimonial committee, edited the souvenir brochure and even drew the picture of him on the cover. It's an interesting reflection on the team spirit of that Cliff Britton/Terry Neill era that so many of the players stayed around long enough to earn testimonials, including Andy Davidson, Malcolm Lord and the great Chris Chilton. It's even more impressive that 30 years on, they're still having reunions and I'm chuffed to bits that they keep on inviting me to them. If Peter Taylor's squad are having reunions in 30 years time, he'll have done a good job, though I won't expect an invitation.

'That, briefly, is the Ken Wagstaff I know – a special guy from a special period in the history of the world's greatest football club. Arsenal and Manchester United supporters might find that difficult to believe, but it's none of their business and they wouldn't understand anyway.'

Alan Plater, playwright.

Brian Sands

A supporter of Hull City since 1946, Brian Sands was a regular visitor to Boothferry Park during the Wagstaff Era.

'Waggy's close affinity with the crowd was partly due to the fact that he regularly scored goals. Many of those were against the country's finest 'keepers, like Banks and Bonetti. He was never phased by playing against higher-level opposition. His wonderful skills were there for all to see.

'He'd put himself about and they always found it hard to shove him off the ball. His popularity was probably also due to the fact he was such a character. He always seemed to play with a cheeky smile and it was clear that he enjoyed his football.

'There were many good players at Boothferry Park in those days. Waggy was an exceptional talent and when talking about Hull City history, the names Carter, Wagstaff and Chilton always spring to mind.'

August 2002

Peter Morris

A local boy, who started his playing with a church team at New Houghton, Peter Morris progressed through Mansfield Town's nursery team Ladybrook Colts. He made his debut against Workington in February 1961. In 364 appearances for the Stags, he scored 53 goals. Almost seven years to the day following his debut, the midfielder moved to Ipswich Town and played successively under managers Bill McGarry and Bobby Robson. Before a successful return to Field Mill as manager in 1976, he had a spell at Norwich City under John Bond. He currently manages King's Lynn having spent time as manager with Peterborough United and Southend.

'Raich Carter played a big centre half with two wingers and two wing-backs. He wanted to get it wide and then fire crosses in to big Roy Chapman and Waggy – a similar partnership to that which developed with Chris Chilton at Hull later in Ken's career.

'Waggy was largely self-taught – a player with a natural ability. A brilliant passer of the ball, his ability shone through. The ball seemed as if it was stuck to his feet when he went past defenders. It was a joy to see a boy of seventeen controlling games and scoring winners. The crowd loved him and the gates reflected his drawing power.

'One year in particular there were loads of penalties. He won them and I scored them. He was an artist at persuading the referee he'd been fouled, a skill he had learned from Raich. That said, he used to get knocked about quite a lot by defenders.'

August 2002

Brian Phillips

Having been recruited from non-League football, Brian Phillips enjoyed a period at Middlesbrough as a player alongside Brian Clough. He transferred to Mansfield in summer 1960 and played more than 100 games for the Stags.

'Waggy made rapid progress after he joined Mansfield and came on came in leaps and bounds. He had tremendous confidence. He was the best striker I ever played with. In fact, given that the likes of Brian Clough and Alan Peacock played for England, Waggy had every right to be capped.

'One of the distinctive features in his play was the technique of laying the ball off with his chest. It's done a lot these days, but wasn't in the 1960s. As a defender, I could see that the only chance of stopping him was to let him turn after receiving the ball and then have a go. If he had his back to you, that was it, he'd be past you. Facing him, at least you had the chance to smack him!

'I was captain of the team and I remember having him by the throat a few times when he used to take the piss in training. After he'd dribbled past a few times he'd make cheeky comments. Still, I got on with him fine. We'd go for a drink together after the games. In fact, the locals used to be amazed. Waggy and I would get off the pitch, out of the bath and into the pub before even the spectators had arrived in there!

'Unfortunately, his reputation as a drinker went before him. People like Joe Mercer at Manchester City looked at signing him but I guess they were put off by some of the stories – many of which were highly exaggerated.'

August 2002

Sammy Chapman

A former player with Manchester United, Sammy Chapman first joined the Stags in 1956. After a spell at Portsmouth, Raich Carter brought him back to Field Mill in 1961. For a period, during the promotion year, he assumed the team captaincy. Currently, he is involved as a scout with David Platt at England Under-21 level.

'Waggy was a damn good player with a wonderful touch on the ball. At first, he played on the wing at Mansfield. I didn't think that suited him. He was quick but not fast enough in that role. However, Raich Carter was adamant that he had a rare talent. In pre-season we played Derby behind closed doors and got stuffed. In a return match Waggy was played in a central striking role. He had a fantastic game. Thereafter, he was mostly played down the centre and went from strength to strength. Raich played a key role in giving him a chance, having faith in him and giving him good advice.'

August 2002

Michael Stringfellow

Nuncargate-born Michael Stringfellow was spotted in local schools football and made his Stags debut with Ken Wagstaff at Rochdale. A skilful winger, he moved to Leicester City for £20,000 in January 1962 and carved out a successful career at Filbert Street. In 12 years, he made 250 appearances with 100 goals to his credit. An

extremely brave player, he sustained a serious injury in 1969 but remained at the club for a further five years.

'Waggy was supremely confident to the point of being cocky. He had great confidence in his own ability and that was important. We made our debuts together at Rochdale and after that I saw him score loads of goals. He missed a few, but that never got him down. Its no use having doubts and letting misses affect your play. He just got on with it and made sure the next chance went in.

'Raich Carter had a simple philosophy. It was that he wanted the forwards to be skilful and be able to play. It was the job of the rest of the team to get the ball to them. Waggy could play and we made sure we got the ball to him! There were a few characters in the Mansfield side at that time. Kenny Wagstaff was the biggest character of them all! He was a natural talent and it is mind-boggling that he never played for England.'

David Coates
Although Newcastle-born David Coates joined Hull City in 1952, his career was temporarily suspended until 1955 as a result of National Service. He moved to Mansfield Town in March 1960. As a Stags player, he made 159 League appearances. Following a move to Notts County in 1964 he became involved in coaching at that club, and then later at Mansfield, Aston Villa, Leicester, Luton and Oxford United. He is currently involved in scouting for Portsmouth and works as a matchday observer for the FA Academy.

Following the successful FA Cup run of 1965/66, the Tigers' skipper Andy Davidson displays the Giant-Killer Cup.

'Certainly, Ken Wagstaff was the best player I ever played with. He was a happy-go-lucky character and a complete player, except he rarely headed the ball. At Mansfield, Peter Morris once said that he didn't need to head the ball. He was probably the most unselfish forward I have ever come up against. He scored a fantastic amount of goals, but he made even more for others.

'Waggy was a character with immense skill. He could turn you inside out in training and make you look stupid with his footwork. He'd chuckle as he went past, but you laughed with him. It didn't cause offence. At Mansfield, Ken was universally liked by all his colleagues and idolised by the crowd. Without doubt he was Raich Carter's protégé. Before he died, Raich himself confided that "Waggy would have been better signing for another club where his chances of international honours would have been greater. Had he gone to Derby County, for example, he would have certainly played for England."'

Andy Davidson

Lanarkshire-born Andy Davidson joined Hull City in 1947. A natural leader and tough defender he made the full-back spot his own and went on to captain the side. He is the current holder of the club's appearance record. Having retired from playing, he continued his involvement with the club for a while in a coaching capacity.

'In my career, I played against many great players – including Stanley Matthews, Tommy Laughton, Tom Finney and others. In my humble opinion, Ken Wagstaff was a better player than any of those. If I had to pick an all time great side, he'd be in it.

'In the box, everything seems to happen at 100 miles an hour. That's too fast for most players. Waggy had lightning reactions coupled with ice-cool thinking. Chris Chilton was a good player and goalscorer. He helped by winning the ball, but Waggy was the ultimate finisher.

'I remember playing at Bristol City on 23 January 1965. It was like the Alamo. We were besieged for most of the game. Waggy was up on the halfway line and had a centre half and sweeper marking him. We only got the ball out of our half about twice in the entire game and he scored on both occasions. After his first goal, they put an extra man on him! In the end, we won the game 2-1.

He was deceptively fast and just left people in his wake. The margin he'd beat them by increased as he got his momentum up. He should have played for England and would have done so had he played in a higher division. It seemed he was happy at Hull City.

'I was friendly with Don Revie at Leeds and he was desperate for his signature. He asked me to persuade him to move. When Waggy refused, he signed Allan Clarke instead. Joe Harvey from Newcastle was also interested.

'Ken has a very dry sense of humour. He always kept well clear of trouble and let his football do the talking. He had a very sensitive side. When the defenders chopped him, he'd just get up and get on with it. I remember on a few occasions warning opposition players what might happen if they went over the top. I think that kept back the worst excesses.

'There will never be another Ken Wagstaff at Hull City. That sort of talent would cost millions these days.'

September 2002

Ken Houghton

Ken Houghton started his working life at Silverwood pit. He played for the colliery team before signing as an amateur with Rotherham United in 1959. As a first-team professional at Millmoor, he quickly established a reputation as a powerful goalscorer with great passing ability and vision. After being headhunted by Cliff Britton, he made his debut for Hull City on 9 January 1965 against Bournemouth.

He was an integral part of the 1960s' 'famous five' forward line, providing a commanding presence and linking up with his former Rotherham colleague and City left winger Ian Butler. He regularly found the net himself, but his intelligent play frequently opened up defences and created opportunities for the Wagstaff and Chilton scoring machine.

In June 1973, he moved to Scunthorpe United and later joined Scarborough as player-coach where he helped the side to a Wembley appearance in the FA Trophy. Later, via Bridlington Town, he returned to Hull City to carry out various roles – including a spell as manager in the late 1970s. He is regarded by many as an intelligent and authoritative voice on football matters, occasionally assists with match radio commentaries and still lives in the Hull area.

'Under Cliff Britton, we were a very disciplined playing side. Waggy was a strong and very quick player with amazing scoring abilities. People often say he was exceptional at close range, but he also scored from long range. I remember one game when he'd seen the 'keeper off his line and scored from just inside the halfway line – close to the dugout!

'They were really good times at Hull City and we had a very good team. But for a little team strengthening, we could have made Division One just after promotion from the Third. Later, under Terry Neil we came close again in the early 1970s. Bringing in younger players had some advantages, but the side lost the discipline and understandings forged under Cliff Britton and it gradually slipped away.

'I rated Ken Wagstaff on a par with the likes of Jimmy Greaves and Denis Law. He was a naturally talented goalscorer. If he was playing today, there is little doubt he'd find a place in most Premiership sides commanding a fee easily in the region of £5 million or more. Obviously, the right partner would help, but someone like van Nistelrooy would be one obvious choice.'

August 2002

Ian Butler

Born in Darton, Ian Butler came through the ranks at Rotherham United before joining Hull City on New Year's Day 1965. He was an exceptionally fast and tricky winger, who provided first-class service to the strikers and at the same time found the net himself whenever the opportunities arose – in fact on 99 occasions throughout his League career. Perhaps his most significant goal came at Boothferry Park on 20 May 1966 in front of 30,371 ecstatic fans when his strike clinched the Division Three championship against Southend United. Finally, he moved to York City in July 1973.

Chillo and Waggy. During the early 1990s Chris Chilton and Ken Wagstaff collaborated on the production of a video containing footage of their Hull City goals. The video featured the lethal twosome talking about their partnership.

Pictured in 1992 at Boothferry Park, Chris Chilton and Ken Wagstaff take a gentle stroll down memory lane.

'I remember transferring from Rotherham to Hull. Suddenly, the manager came round to my house and said: "Come on, you're going to Hull." He reassured me that they were going places and told me about Ken Wagstaff and Chris Chilton. I already knew Waggy from our days with Rotherham juniors.

'Cliff Britton took me and the family out for a meal at the Royal Station Hotel and welcomed us to the City. Just before we went in, I noticed the newspaper placards noting that they had paid £40,000. Until that moment, I hadn't a clue what the fee had been. The next day, I played in my debut against Colchester United at Boothferry Park. I didn't score in that game but I didn't have to because we won 5-1.

'Waggy was the ultimate scoring machine. He had superb control and composure – hitting the target almost every time. There were lots of stories about his drinking, but frankly they were mostly rubbish. He liked a drink, but he was so determined, he'd run it off in training the next day. We never drank before a game. Once, coming home from a tour abroad on the ferry, Terry Neil had banned drinking. Then, Tommy Docherty, his assistant, discovered that he'd got the Scottish manager's job. We found him in the bar buying all the drinks. Before long, he was serving behind the bar and we were all singing the "Sheikh of Araby"! In fact, by the time the celebrations had finished, the boat had been docked three hours!

'Waggy used to come up with bright ideas from time to time. Once he hit on this brainwave that when I got the ball he would point to where he wanted it without the defender knowing. The first time he did it, I saw this little furtive signal to the right. I slotted it through and blow me he ran to the left. The crowd shouted "Come on Butler sort yourself out." I never ever found out whether it was Waggy's little wind-up or whether he'd confused himself but I never took any more chances after that.'

August 2002

Chris Chilton

Sproatley-born Chris Chilton joined Hull City in 1959, making his first-team debut against Colchester United on 20 August 1960. He was an exceptional goalscoring talent and remains the holder of the club's goalscoring record. His partnership with Ken Wagstaff was awesome.

Like Waggy, Chris Chilton was an international-quality player, but the captaincy of an FA XI marked the pinnacle of his career at that level. He and Waggy toured Australasia in 1971 with the FA, but shortly afterwards Chillo moved to Coventry for around £92,000 amid rumours of a deteriorating relationship with manager Terry Neil and his assistant Tommy Docherty.

In the folklore of Hull City the names Chilton, Wagstaff and Carter spring almost immediately to mind. Chris Chilton was greatly respected by his playing colleagues as an inspirational character. In later years when he returned to the club as assistant manager, his exceptional qualities as a man-manager were recognised.

'When Ken arrived at Hull, we hit it off straight away. Although I scored a lot of goals, I didn't regard myself as a goalscorer! Waggy and I had this understanding and it worked both ways. I'd tend to work as a decoy drawing defenders away from him. If there was a reasonable chance of scoring, then I'd have a go but if it wasn't on, the next thought was – where is he?

'I always say that if they had combined both of us into one, then you'd probably have the ideal player. My particular strengths were in the air with the ability to run and shoot. I'd learned how to jump for a ball and at the top to rise again even higher and stay there for that second longer to win the ball and direct it either goalwards or to another player. My heading technique recognised that the ball already arrives at speed. Therefore, the main emphasis is on using that momentum and directing it to the target by facing the objective.

'Waggy had exceptional talent in reading the game. He had clinical finishing ability – a very strong player with fantastic control. Ken and I got on exceptionally well off the field as well. There was a mutual respect and it was a pleasure playing for Hull City in those years. The crowd were good to us and we enjoyed a good measure of success with the players put together by Cliff Britton.'

August 2002

Malcolm Lord

Over a 16-year period, Malcolm Lord made 344 appearances for Hull City. His solid and reliable style contributed immensely to the overall team performance. Named Supporters' Player of the Year in 1977, he scored a notable hat-trick in a 4-1 win over Burnley in March 1977.

It was perhaps the general spectre of football managers being sacked with alarming regularity that persuaded him to follow a career outside football – despite being a qualified FA coach.

'Chillo and Waggy were big men. Waggy didn't look quick but was deceptive. He had fantastic strength on the ball. Once he'd got it, they couldn't knock him off. I used to watch the team when I played in the juniors. We'd finish our game and then rush along to Boothferry Park to catch the last 20 minutes of the second half in the 1965/66 promotion year. They came very close to going up again.

'Later when I joined the side I found myself playing alongside the players I'd watched as a junior. The idea was to get the ball forward as quickly as possible to Chillo and Waggy. There were several options and Ian Butler was well capable of scoring. Cliff Britton's system was copied by Graham Taylor when he took Watford from Division Four to the First.

'In the early 1970s we came very close to achieving Division One football. It just went off the boil towards the end of that 1970/71 season. Terry Neil basically took over Cliff's system and tinkered with it a bit. Later, different players came in and it slipped.'

August 2002

John Hawley

Plucked from East Riding Junior football, John Hawley made his debut for Hull City in April 1973. He was a classy player with a string of spectacular goals to his credit. Eventually moving on to play for Leeds, Sunderland, Arsenal and Leyton Orient, he returned on loan to the Tigers in December 1982.

'One of the most startling things I ever saw on a football pitch was in a goalmouth incident involving Ken Wagstaff. He'd been out through injuries towards the end of his career and was unusually playing in the reserves. He was in the box with a clutch of defenders when the ball ricocheted skywards. It was in the air on a trajectory that was moving away from the goal.

The defenders followed that curve. Waggy did the opposite. In fact, once it hit the pitch, the ball landed and swung towards his waiting boot. A split second later it was in the net. In judging his position, he'd actually seen the backspin on the ball. It was awesome.

'He also had a cheeky sense of humour. One day we'd been out on a run down Anlaby road and round the nearby Pickering Park. On our way back to Boothferry Park, I was one of the laggards struggling along. Suddenly, we were overtaken by a milk float. Reclining on the back among the crates was Waggy – swigging from a pint of milk!'

August 2002

John McSeveney

Before joining Hull City, John McSeveney had spells with Hamilton, Sunderland, Cardiff City and Newport. Having turned in more than 400 career League appearances, he turned his hand to coaching and management. While at Hull City he operated on both flanks and during the 1962/63 season scored 22 goals from 39 games. He is currently involved in scouting for Manchester United.

'The teamwork between Ken Wagstaff and Chris Chilton was almost telepathic. Cliff Britton had an attacking philosophy built around a centre forward. Originally, he intended to build the team around Chillo, but to blend in the others was a stroke of genius. It's hard to pick out a favourite Waggy goal because they were all gems. He reminded me very much of John Charles – a man who could run with the ball, control it and pass with a silky touch.

'Chillo and Waggy would spend at least 18 minutes in the box every day in training. Later, other players would follow on in that system, like Stuart Pearson, Paddy Greenwood, John Hawley and Jeff Hemmerman – all of whom went on to carve out successful careers.

'Waggy had a bit of a reputation with the fans as a drinker. Certainly, he liked to socialise. There are some interesting stories – but they are mostly exaggerated. It's a problem for footballers in particular because they are in the public eye. I remember when I was a player at Newport, I'd had a bit of a barney with manager Billy Lucas. In the end, it blew over and he said: "Come on John, I'll buy you a pint." When we arrived at the pub he ordered two halves and placed them a foot apart on the bar. I asked him why he'd bought

Ken Wagstaff pictured shortly after signing for Hull City.

me a half despite having promised me a pint. He replied: "You've got your pint there. If you are seen to be drinking halves, the fans will say you are a steady drinker. If they see you with pints, they'll say you are a piss artist!" That was a brilliant lesson learned.

'Jimmy Lodge, the long-serving physiotherapist was a real character. As coach, after my playing days were over, Jimmy and I worked closely together. He came to me one day and told me that Waggy had been asking for extra massage before the game. I was a little concerned that it would be a regular thing, but told Jimmy to just keep him happy.

'After the game had kicked off, I noticed Waggy scratching himself in strange places where the sun doesn't shine. I looked around and saw Jimmy in the tunnel laughing like one of those cartoon characters and winking at me. In the massage oil he'd deliberately overdone the spicy component. Poor old Waggy was jumping around like a cat on a hot tin roof!

August 2002

Ray Henderson

Ashington-born Ray Henderson played for Middlesbrough before transferring to Hull City in June 1961. He made 226 League appearances for the Tigers and scored 54 League goals. Although remembered as a winger, he also operated as a right-sided midfield player or inside forward. After leaving the Tigers in October 1968, he went on to be player-coach at Reading before taking up various management roles at Everton and Southport. Eventually, he left the game and took up a management job in a Yorkshire engineering firm.

'When you look at supremely talented players you see special skills. Waggy had the ability to go past players and score. His brand of magic could open up teams.

'On 9 April 1966 we played a game at Brentford. It was our second game in two days. The previous day it had been a baking hot day. Afterwards, there had been thunderstorms. It was a beautifully fresh day as we walked around the pitch just before the game. Waggy said he felt good. Then he said to me: "Hendy, four today." I asked him if he meant we'd get four. He replied: "No, I'm going to get four." The result that day was 4-2 to us. All four goals were scored by Ken Wagstaff.

'It didn't end there. The following October we were sitting in the dressing room at Cardiff City. He said it again: "Hendy – Brentford." I asked him if he meant we'd get four. He gave me exactly the same reply as at Brentford: "No Hendy, I'll get four." In fact the record shows the score Hull City 4 Cardiff City 2 – with all four goals scored by Wagstaff! Even in Wagstaff terms it was rare to score four goals, but to predict it before the match was spooky. He was supremely confident and just felt good on those days I guess. My role was to support Waggy and Chillo and cover back for Andy Davidson at full-back when he'd come forward. Cliff Britton was a tactical master and played a specific system. They talk about wing-backs years later but Cliff Britton used similar tactics in the 1960s.

'I remember playing in front of a poor gate once with Andy Davidson. There was only a sprinkling of fans in the east stand when the ball bounced its way up to this chap who was red faced with rage. He'd been shouting abuse for most of the match. Andy went

to take the throw-in and this bloke shouted: "Davidson you're fucking useless." Andy was a tough bloke and he shouted back: "I'm going to remember your face and thump your fucking brains out after the match." The next time the ball went out, I took the throw and I heard the same bloke shout: "Henderson you're fucking useless." It seemed I'd taken the abuse away from Andy. We both roared with laughter after the game. Waggy was always the crowd-pleasing favourite. He never got that sort of flack!'
August 2002

Ian McKechnie

Ian McKechnie joined the Tigers in August 1966 and played alongside Ken Wagstaff until 1974 – making 255 League appearances. In fact, he'd also faced Waggy as an opponent on three occasions while playing as a 'keeper with Southend United. Now living in a beautiful country cottage not far from Hull, in typical jovial fashion and with a familiar Scottish brogue, he recounted some of his memories of Ken.

'Waggy and Chillo used to do their utmost to imprint me on the wall of the training centre during shooting practice! I got on well with Waggy, though sometimes he could be a little short with people. However, his foibles pale into insignificance when you realise how brilliant a player he was. He seemed to have a way of scoring goals and making them look very simple, whereas in actual fact they weren't. Playing in tandem with Chillo, he used to take up the most brilliant positions but he also got immaculate service from Chillo.

'His finishing was clinical except on the odd occasion when he took the mickey and you'd say: "Go on, get the ball in the net!" I recall one particular goal he scored. It was one of the best goals I've ever seen for its audacity because he could have scored about five minutes before he did. We were playing Burnley on a wet day at Turf Moor. The scores were even, very near to the end of the game. Burnley won a corner and as I went for it, the ball started to go away. By the time I'd finished following through, I was almost on the edge of the box. I just got a hand to it and flapped it down and away.

'I think it went to Frank Banks who played it through to Waggy down the centre, just short of the halfway line, with two Burnley defenders close by. Waggy did his usual trick, dropping a shoulder one way and then going in the other direction. Both defenders fell for it and a gap opened up. Ken just dashed through and steamed off looking like a hippo in the mud chasing a ball with the defenders running after him. As Alan Stephenson dashed out, Waggy dropped his shoulder again. The goalie went one way and Waggy and the ball went the other way.

'One of the defenders sussed what was happening and ran towards to the goal line while the other one chased Waggy, who was now wide of the goal to the left. Turning, he pulled the ball away from the defender who'd committed himself to the tackle and left him stranded as he headed back again towards the centre. The other defender came out again and fell for the same dummy as Waggy dribbled round him and the goalie. I swear he stood with his foot on the ball right on the goal line and just rolled it into the net! That was the man.'
August 2002

Mick Brown

Born in Walsall, Mick Brown came to Hull City through Gloucester schools football in July 1954. He signed professional forms in October 1958 and made his debut in October 1959. His career progressed with a move to Lincoln in July 1967 and then to Cambridge as player-coach in May 1968. Thereafter, he held a number of posts with Oxford, West Brom, Manchester United and Bolton Wanderers. He worked closely with Ron Atkinson during his tenure at Old Trafford and is currently Chief Scout with the club.

'When Ken Wagstaff came to Hull City, I was unofficially appointed to show him the ropes. Someone just said: "Browny, keep an eye on him." It was a hell of a job! Ideally, it would have taken the British Armed Forces to have done that! We went out for "a drink" one night in Hull.

'After a while, I'd had it. I couldn't stand up but Waggy was completely unaffected. He said: "Let's go for one in Smokey Joe's" – or something similar. I was puzzled, because I didn't know where it was. It turned out it was in Mansfield and I believe he got a lift and went!

'I was a friend of David Coates and when he went to Mansfield, I used to go over there to watch the games. That's when I first saw Waggy in action, scoring goal after goal for the Stags. He was a fantastic talent. Then, he came to Hull and with Chris Chilton became part of the club's folklore. They were chalk and cheese as individuals, but as a strike partnership they were fantastic. It is sad that they didn't play together in Division One. They were well capable of it along with Ian Butler. It was a team of top-quality players.

'Waggy had the ability to see things that others couldn't. He was on a different level with great perception and supreme confidence in his own ability. You could compare him on a level with Di Canio in the present game in that he could create something out of nothing. He was amazingly cool inside the box.

As for his ability to persuade the referees to award free-kicks, I'm only glad that I didn't have to play against him. I would have spent more time walking down the tunnel. He had a knack of edging back into the centre half then suddenly lurching forward as if poleaxed!

'People often try to compare Waggy to Jimmy Greaves. Although Ken was quick, he was supreme at beating defenders by deception. Perhaps Greavesy had a little more pace and enjoyed playing at a higher level. However, when it came to scoring goals they were on a par. Both had great self-belief. To them, scoring was almost a normal state of affairs – nothing unusual.'

August 2002

John Kaye

Brought to Hull City as a player by Terry Neil in November 1971, John Kaye had already enjoyed a long and successful spell with West Bromwich Albion. Having joined that club in 1963 from Scunthorpe United, he won an FA Cup winners' medal and a Football League Cup winners' medal. The side had been runners up in 1967 and 1970. His skill and experience in midfield brought strength to the Tigers' defence. A serious knee injury curtailed his playing career in 1973 but led to his continuing involvement with the club in a coaching capacity. Shortly afterwards, he became manager when Neil transferred to Spurs. His tenure lasted until 1977.

'Ken was a legend in football. He averaged a goal in every other game in the League in a career that spanned more than 500 matches. He was a complete master of all the basic football skills and did things simply and quickly. His control on the ball was fantastic and he had the ability to go past defenders by deception.

'Without doubt, he was an unselfish player with fantastic vision and a very astute football brain. He read the game extremely well and but for his abilities as a forward, his creativity and passing ability would have made him a great asset in midfield. In the latter part of his career, Ken had two serious operations. He bounced back in a way that took guts and hard work. Always the target for robust defenders, he took the tackles, shirt pulling and fouls without retaliation. He'd simply get up and get on with the game.

'Ken was a hard taskmaster and expected fellow players to play up to his high standard. Otherwise, he'd let them know in no uncertain terms. One or two thought he was a bit abrupt but in fact he was only trying to get them to play better. It was the same with the referees. He'd tell them what he thought and if things weren't right he'd have a good old moan. In terms of his goalscoring abilities I would put Ken Wagstaff on a par with the great Jimmy Greaves – one of the best all-time players in the game. Waggy had deceptive pace. He looked slow until you tried to stay up with him!

'At the end of the day, he was enthusiastic, exceptionally talented, proud of his ability and loved the game. I never fully understood why he didn't push harder to get into a bigger club. Not only would it have almost guaranteed him an England place but he would have also earned significantly more money. I couldn't believe the poor salaries players were earning when I came to the club.

'My own view is that he was settled at Hull City because he was appreciated by the fans. That adulation counts for a lot and there's no guarantee it will happen at a bigger club in quite the same way. However, his talent would have graced any team in the country. One or two of the other players could also have moved up. I wasn't surprised to see Chris Chilton move on to Coventry. These days they would be paid astronomical salaries in comparison to what they were earning then.'

August 2002

Farrell and Carter. FA Cup, 6 January 1951. Hull City 2 Everton 0.

In Memory of Raich Carter

Horatio Stratton Carter was the man who brought a youthful Ken Wagstaff from the obscurity of a Nottinghamshire playing field into the professional game of football. In the space of a single match, from the jaws of frenetic action and in the midst of twenty-two players with kindred spirit, he plucked a talent, the rarity of which could only be determined so decisively and prophetically by a man who himself possessed such qualities.

Carter was an England international, a football aristocrat, whose silky skills earned him the title 'maestro'. A player with Sunderland, Derby County and Hull City, he also managed that club before taking the reins at Leeds United and then Mansfield Town and Middlesbrough. His honours as a player included FA Cup Finals and League Championships. In every sense, he was one of football's all-time greats.

In the autumn of his life, Carter maintained close contact with those players whom he had reared in the game. But as the great man's life flickered towards the end, his voice was all but silenced by the illness that eventually took his life. In the final days he was visited by the players he had moulded.

Still with humour intact, despite great grief, Ken Wagstaff held his hand and spoke comforting words about glory days past. It was mentor and protégé, together for the last time. They were poignant moments in the company of David Coates, Peter Morris and Brian Phillips. After the men had gone, a nurse talked to the great man about his visitors. With the only words he could muster, Carter replied: 'My boys.'

John Maffin
August 2002

Above: Raich Carter pictured in Hull City colours.

RAICH CARTER

1990s photograph showing ex-Tigers at Boothferry Park.

Bibliography

D. Bond	(1999)	*Hull City*	Breedon Books
C. Elton	(1999)	*Hull City Football Club*	Tempus
C. Elton	(1989)	*Hull City: A Complete Record*	Breedon Books
J. Lovejoy	(1999)	*Bestie*	Pan
C. Miller	(1998)	*He Always Puts It To The Right*	Orion
M. Peterson	(1998)	*The Definitive Hull City AFC*	Tony Brown
M. Peterson	(2000)	*Tiger Tales*	Yore
S. Searle	(1991)	*Mansfield Town: A Complete Record 1910–1990*	Breedon Books

Waggy sends the 'keeper the wrong way.

Appendices

Ken Wagstaff's Hull City Career and Appearances

Season	League Apps	Gls	FA Cup Apps	Gls	FL Cup Apps	Gls	Others Apps	Gls	Total Apps	Gls
1964/65	25	23	2	0	0	0			27	23
1965/66	46	27	7	3	2	1			55	31
1966/67	39	21	3	0	1	0			43	21
1967/68	40	17	3	2	1	1			44	20
1968/69	39	20	1	0	2	1			42	21
1969/70	38	18	1	0	2	1			41	19
1970/71	38	12	4	4	1	0	2	2	45	18
1971/72	32	11	3	3	1	0			36	14
1972/73	(3) 13	4	2	1	1	0	1	0	(3) 17	5
1973/74	32	8	2	0	5	2	3	0	42	10
1974/75	23	10	1	1	1	0			25	11
1975/76	(1) 9	2	0	0	2	0	(1) 1	2	(2) 12	4
TOTAL	(4) 374	173	29	14	19	6	(1) 7	4	(5) 429	197

Source: *Hull City: A Complete Record* 1989 Chris Elton (Breedon Books)

Mansfield Town Career and Appearances

Season	League Apps	Gls	FA Cup Apps	Gls	FL Cup Apps	Gls	Others Apps	Gls	Total Apps	Gls
1960/61	27	9	0	0	0	0			27	9
1961/62	42	12	2	0	3	3			47	15
1962/63	44	34	5	7	0	0			49	41
1963/64	46	29	1	0	2	0			49	29
1964/65	22	9	0	0	2	2			24	11
TOTAL	181*	93	8	7	7	5			196	105

*One match *v.* Accrington Stanley expunged

Source: *Mansfield Town: A Complete Record 1910-1990* Stan Searle (Breedon Books)

Waggy – Club by Club [Hull City Career]

Opponent	League		FA Cup		FL Cup		Other Comps	
	Apps.	Gls	Apps.	Gls	Apps.	Gls	Apps.	Gls
AFC Bournemouth	4	2	-	-	-	-	-	-
Aston Villa	9	5	-	-	-	-	-	-
Bari	-	-	-	-	-	-	1	-
Birmingham City	10	3	-	-	-	-	-	-
Blackburn Rovers	10	2	-	-	-	-	-	-
Blackpool	11	1	1	1	-	-	-	-
Bolton Wanderers	12	5	-	-	-	-	-	-
Bradford P.A.	-	-	1	-	-	-	-	-
Brentford	3	5	1	-	1	-	-	-
Brighton & H.A.	4	2	-	-	-	-	-	-
Bristol City	16	7	2	-	-	-	-	-
Bristol Rovers	5	2	-	-	-	-	1	-
Burnley	2	1	-	-	1	-	-	-
Bury	3	5	-	-	-	-	-	-
Cardiff City	17	10	-	-	-	-	-	-
Carlisle Utd	16	3	-	-	-	-	-	-
Charlton Athletic	10	5	1	1	-	-	-	-
Chelsea	1	-	2	2	-	-	-	-
Colchester Utd	1	2	-	-	-	-	-	-
Coventry City	2	-	1	1	-	-	-	-
Crystal Palace	7	2	-	-	-	-	-	-
Derby County	6	2	-	-	3	1	-	-
Doncaster Rovers	-	-	-	-	1	-	-	-
Exeter City	4	3	-	-	-	-	-	-
Fulham	5	5	1	1	-	-	-	-
Gateshead	-	-	1	1	-	-	-	-
Gillingham	3	3	-	-	-	-	-	-
Grimsby Town	3	3	-	-	-	-	-	-
Halifax	-	-	-	-	1	1	-	-
Huddersfield Town	10	3	-	-	-	-	-	-
Ipswich Town	4	2	-	-	-	-	-	-
Leicester City	3	2	-	-	2	1	-	-
Leyton Orient	5	2	-	-	-	-	-	-
Lincoln City	-	-	2	-	1	-	-	-
Liverpool	-	-	-	-	3	-	-	-
Luton Town	6	1	-	-	-	-	-	-
Manchester City	-	-	1	-	-	-	-	-
Manchester Utd	1	1	-	-	-	-	1	-
Mansfield Town	3	3	-	-	-	-	2	1
Middlesbrough	12	4	3	2	-	-	-	-

Opponent	League		FA Cup		FL Cup		Other Comps	
	Apps.	Gls	Apps.	Gls	Apps.	Gls	Apps.	Gls
Millwall	15	5	-	-	-	-	-	-
Northampton Town	2	2	-	-	-	-	-	-
Norwich City	13	4	1	1	2	1	-	-
Nottingham Forest	4	1	1	-	-	-	-	-
Notts County	3	2	-	-	-	-	-	-
Oldham A	5	3	-	-	-	-	-	-
Oxford Utd	13	5	-	-	-	-	-	-
Peterborough Utd	3	1	-	-	-	-	1	2
Plymouth Argyle	4	3	-	-	-	-	-	-
Port Vale	2	4	-	-	-	-	-	-
Portsmouth	15	7	3	-	-	-	-	-
Preston North End	10	6	-	-	-	-	-	-
QPR	10	4	-	-	1	1	-	-
Reading	2	-	-	-	-	-	-	-
Rotherham Utd	3	-	-	-	-	-	-	-
Scunthorpe Utd	2	2	-	-	-	-	-	-
Sheffield Utd	5	5	-	-	1	-	-	-
Sheffield Wednesday	7	2	-	-	-	-	-	-
Shrewsbury Town	3	1	-	-	-	-	-	-
Southampton	3	2	1	-	-	-	-	-
Southend Utd	4	-	-	-	-	-	-	-
Southport	-	-	1	-	-	-	-	-
Stockport County	-	-	2	1	1	1	-	-
Stoke City	-	-	2	3	-	-	1	-
Sunderland	7	3	-	-	-	-	-	-
Swansea City	2	2	-	-	-	-	-	-
Swindon Town	9	3	-	-	-	-	-	-
Walsall	3	2	-	-	-	-	-	-
Watford	9	4	-	-	-	-	-	-
West Brom	4	2	-	-	-	-	1	1
West Ham Utd	-	-	-	-	1	-	-	-
Wolves	2	-	1	-	-	-	-	-
Workington	3	1	-	-	-	-	-	-
York City	3	1	-	-	-	-	-	-
Total	378	173	29	14	19	6	8	4